NONTECHNICAL STRATEGIES TO REDUCE CHILDREN'S EXPOSURE TO INAPPROPRIATE MATERIAL ON THE INTERNET

SUMMARY OF A WORKSHOP

Committee to Study Tools and Strategies for
Protecting Kids from Pornography and Their Applicability to
Other Inappropriate Internet Content

Joah G. Iannotta, Editor

Board on Children, Youth, and Families
and
Computer Science and Telecommunications Board

Division of Behavioral and Social Sciences and Education
and
Division on Engineering and Physical Sciences

National Research Council
and
Institute of Medicine

NATIONAL ACADEMY PRESS
Washington, D.C.

NATIONAL ACADEMY PRESS 2101 Constitution Avenue, N.W. Washington, D.C. 20418

NOTICE: The project that is the subject of this report was approved by the Governing Board of the National Research Council, whose members are drawn from the councils of the National Academy of Sciences, the National Academy of Engineering, and the Institute of Medicine. The members of the committee responsible for the report were chosen for their special competences and with regard for appropriate balance.

The study of which this workshop report was a part was supported by Grant No. 1999-JN-FX-0071 between the National Academy of Sciences and the U.S. Departments of Justice and Education; Grant No. P0073380 between the National Academy of Sciences and the W.K. Kellogg Foundation; awards (unnumbered) from the Microsoft Corporation and IBM; and National Research Council funds. Any opinions, findings, conclusions, or recommendations expressed in this publication are those of the author(s) and do not necessarily reflect the views of the organizations or agencies that provided support for this project.

International Standard Book Number 0-309-07591-2

Additional copies of this report are available from the National Academy Press, 2101 Constitution Avenue, N.W., Lock Box 285, Washington, D.C. 20055.

Call (800) 624-6242 or (202) 334-3313 (in the Washington metropolitan area)

This report is also available online at http://www.nap.edu

Printed in the United States of America

Copyright 2001 by the National Academy of Sciences. All rights reserved.

Suggested citation: National Research Council and Institute of Medicine, 2001. *Nontechnical Strategies to Reduce Children's Exposure to Inappropriate Material on the Internet: Summary of a Workshop*. Board on Children, Youth, and Families and Computer Science and Telecommunications Board. Joah G. Iannotta, ed. Washington, D.C.: National Academy Press.

THE NATIONAL ACADEMIES

National Academy of Sciences
National Academy of Engineering
Institute of Medicine
National Research Council

The **National Academy of Sciences** is a private, nonprofit, self-perpetuating society of distinguished scholars engaged in scientific and engineering research, dedicated to the furtherance of science and technology and to their use for the general welfare. Upon the authority of the charter granted to it by the Congress in 1863, the Academy has a mandate that requires it to advise the federal government on scientific and technical matters. Dr. Bruce M. Alberts is president of the National Academy of Sciences.

The **National Academy of Engineering** was established in 1964, under the charter of the National Academy of Sciences, as a parallel organization of outstanding engineers. It is autonomous in its administration and in the selection of its members, sharing with the National Academy of Sciences the responsibility for advising the federal government. The National Academy of Engineering also sponsors engineering programs aimed at meeting national needs, encourages education and research, and recognizes the superior achievements of engineers. Dr. William A. Wulf is president of the National Academy of Engineering.

The **Institute of Medicine** was established in 1970 by the National Academy of Sciences to secure the services of eminent members of appropriate professions in the examination of policy matters pertaining to the health of the public. The Institute acts under the responsibility given to the National Academy of Sciences by its congressional charter to be an adviser to the federal government and, upon its own initiative, to identify issues of medical care, research, and education. Dr. Kenneth I. Shine is president of the Institute of Medicine.

The **National Research Council** was organized by the National Academy of Sciences in 1916 to associate the broad community of science and technology with the Academy's purposes of furthering knowledge and advising the federal government. Functioning in accordance with general policies determined by the Academy, the Council has become the principal operating agency of both the National Academy of Sciences and the National Academy of Engineering in providing services to the government, the public, and the scientific and engineering communities. The Council is administered jointly by both Academies and the Institute of Medicine. Dr. Bruce M. Alberts and Dr. William A. Wulf are chairman and vice chairman, respectively, of the National Research Council.

COMMITTEE TO STUDY TOOLS AND STRATEGIES FOR PROTECTING KIDS FROM PORNOGRAPHY AND THEIR APPLICABILITY TO OTHER INAPPROPRIATE INTERNET CONTENT
2000-2001

RICHARD THORNBURGH (*Chair*), Kirkpatrick & Lockhart LLP, Washington, DC
NICHOLAS J. BELKIN, School of Communication, Information and Library Studies, Rutgers University
REV. WILLIAM J. BYRON, Holy Trinity Church, Washington, DC
SANDRA L. CALVERT, Department of Psychology, Georgetown University
DAVID FORSYTH, Department of Computer Science, University of California, Berkeley
DANIEL GEER, @Stake, Cambridge, MA
LINDA HODGE, National Parent Teacher Association, Washington, DC
MARILYN GELL MASON, Independent Consultant, Tallahassee, FL
MILO MEDIN, Excite@Home, Redwood City, CA
JOHN B. RABURN, National Center for Missing and Exploited Children, Alexandria, VA
ROBIN RASKIN, *FamilyPC Magazine*, New York, NY
ROBERT SCHOLS, T.J. Watson Research Center, IBM, Yorktown Heights, NY
JANET WARD SCHOFIELD, Learning Research and Development Center, University of Pittsburgh
GEOFFREY R. STONE, Office of the Provost, University of Chicago
WINNIE WECHSLER, Independent Consultant, Santa Monica, CA

Herbert Lin, *Senior Scientist*
Gail Pritchard, *Program Officer*
Joah G. Iannotta, *Research Assistant*
Daniel D. Llata, *Senior Project Assistant*

BOARD ON CHILDREN, YOUTH, AND FAMILIES
1999-2000

EVAN CHARNEY (*Chair*), Department of Pediatrics, University of Massachusetts
JAMES A. BANKS, Center for Multicultural Education, University of Washington
SHEILA BURKE, John F. Kennedy School of Government, Harvard University
DAVID CARD, Department of Economics, University of California, Berkeley
DONALD COHEN, Yale-New Haven Children's Hospital, Yale University
MINDY FULLILOVE, Columbia University
KEVIN GRUMBACH, Department of Family and Community Medicine, Primary Care Research Center, University of California, San Francisco
MAXINE HAYES, Department of Community and Family Health, Washington State Department of Health
MARGARET HEAGARTY, Department of Pediatrics, Harlem Hospital Center, Columbia University
RENEE JENKINS, Department of Pediatrics and Child Health, Howard University
SHEILA KAMERMAN, School of Social Work, Columbia University
HARRIET KITZMAN, School of Nursing, University of Rochester
SANDERS KORENMAN, School of Public Affairs, Baruch College
HON. CINDY LEDERMAN, Circuit Court, Juvenile Justice Center, Dade County, Florida
SARA McLANAHAN, Office of Population Research, Princeton University
VONNIE McLOYD, Center for Human Growth and Development, University of Michigan
GARY SANDEFUR, Department of Sociology, University of Wisconsin, Madison
RUTH STEIN, Department of Pediatrics, Albert Einstein College of Medicine
PAUL WISE, Department of Pediatrics, Boston Medical Center

RUTH T. GROSS (*Liaison, IOM Board on Health Promotion and Disease Prevention*), Professor of Pediatrics (emerita), Stanford University
ELEANOR E. MACCOBY (*Liaison, Division of Behavioral and Social Sciences and Education*), Department of Psychology (emerita), Stanford University
WILLIAM ROPER (*Liaison, IOM Council*), Institute of Medicine, University of North Carolina, Chapel Hill

Michele D. Kipke, *Director*

COMPUTER SCIENCE AND TELECOMMUNICATIONS BOARD
1999-2000

DAVID D. CLARK (*Chair*), Laboratory of Computer Science, Massachusetts Institute of Technology
DAVID BORTH, Communication Systems and Technologies Labs, Motorola Labs, Schaumburg, IL
JAMES CHIDDIX, AOL Time Warner, Stamford, CT
JOHN M. CIOFFI, Department of Electrical Engineering, Stanford University
ELAINE COHEN, Department of Computer Science, University of Utah
W. BRUCE CROFT, Center for Intelligent Information Retrieval, University of Massachusetts at Amherst
SUSAN L. GRAHAM, Department of Computer Science, University of California at Berkeley
JUDITH HEMPEL, Molecular Design Institute, University of California at San Francisco
JEFFREY M. JAFFE, Bell Laboratories, Lucent Technologies, Murray Hill, NJ
ANNA KARLIN, Department of Computer Science and Engineering, University of Washington
MICHAEL KATZ, Department of Economics, Haas School of Business, University of California at Berkeley
BUTLER W. LAMPSON, Microsoft Corporation, Cambridge, MA
EDWARD D. LAZOWSKA, Department of Computer Science and Engineering, University of Washington
DAVID LIDDLE, U.S. Venture Partners, Menlo Park, CA
TOM M. MITCHELL, WhizBang! Labs, Inc., Pittsburgh, PA
DONALD NORMAN, UNext.com, Deerfield, IL
DAVID A. PATTERSON, Department of Computer Science, University of California at Berkeley
HENRY (HANK) PERRITT, Chicago-Kent College of Law
CHARLES SIMONYI, Microsoft Corporation, Redmond, WA
BURTON SMITH, Cray Inc., Seattle, WA
TERRY SMITH, Department of Computer Science, University of California at Santa Barbara
LEE SPROULL, Stern School of Management, New York University

Marjory S. Blumenthal, *Executive Director*

Contents

Preface		ix
1	Introduction	1
2	The Context of Strategy Development: The Needs of School and Parents	6
3	Creating a Framework for Developing Effective Nontechnical Strategies	17
4	Nontechnical Strategies	42
5	Research, Policy, and Practice: Future Directions	68
6	Developing Nontechnical Strategies: Concluding Thoughts	76
References		79
Appendix: Workshop Materials		85

Preface

In response to a mandate from Congress in conjunction with the Protection of Children from Sexual Predators Act of 1998, the Computer Science and Telecommunications Board and the Board on Children, Youth, and Families of the National Research Council and the Institute of Medicine established a committee of experts to explore options to protect children from pornography and other inappropriate Internet content. In June 2000, the Committee to Study Tools and Strategies for Protecting Kids from Pornography on the Internet and Their Applicability to Other Inappropriate Internet Content was established. Support for the committee's work came from the U.S. Department of Education, the U.S. Department of Justice, Microsoft Corporation, IBM, the W.K. Kellogg Foundation, and the National Research Council. The committee has been charged with exploring the pros and cons of different technology options and operational policies as well as nontechnical strategies that can help to provide young people with positive and safe online experiences.

On December 13, 2000, the committee convened a workshop to provide public input to its work and focus on nontechnical strategies that could be effective in a broad range of settings (e.g., home, school, libraries) in which young people might be online. With primary support provided by the W.K. Kellogg Foundation, the Board on Children, Youth, and Families assumed responsibility for planning and organizing the workshop. The workshop brought together researchers, educators, policy makers, and other key stakeholders to consider and discuss these approaches and to identify some of the benefits and limitations of various nontechnical strategies. The workshop was organized around four topics: developmental considerations for defining inappropriate material and the effects of exposure to sexually explicit and other harmful materials; children's use patterns and experiences on the Internet; innovative approaches and existing efforts to use nontechnological strategies; and opportunities to bridge research, policy, and practice. The overarching goal of this activity was to provide a forum for discussing the implications of this research with regard to policy and practice and identifying research needed to advance and inform policy and practice.

This report summarizes the proceedings from the workshop, and, while it offers insight from the presenters on the strengths of nontechnical strategies, it does not contain conclusions or recommendations. Rather, it suggests that the approach or combination of approaches that best serve young people need to be based on the context, needs, and manner in which they are using the Internet. In addition, this report represents a distillation of the presentations of the speakers and the dialogue that ensued, highlighting key issues and viewpoints that emerged from the rich discussions that took place. Every effort has been made to accurately reflect the speakers' content and viewpoints. However, because the report reflects the proceedings of the workshop, it is not intended to be a comprehensive review of all the issues involved in Internet use by young people, nor is it a complete documentation of all the nontechnical strategies that communities, schools, parents, and libraries might use.

This report has been reviewed in draft form by individuals chosen for their diverse perspectives and technical expertise, in accordance with procedures approved by the Report Review Committee of the National Research Council (NRC). The purpose of this independent review is to provide candid and critical comments that will assist the institution in making the published report as sound as possible and to ensure that the report meets institutional standards for objectivity, evidence, and responsiveness to the study charge. The review comments and draft manuscript remain confidential to protect the integrity of the deliberative process.

We thank the following individuals for their participation in the review of this report: Susan Curnan, Center for Youth and Communities, Brandeis University; Sari Feldman, Deputy Director, Cleveland Public Library; Sara Kiesler, Human Computer Interaction Institute, Carnegie Mellon University; and Christine Peterson, SRI International, Arlington, VA.

Although the reviewers listed above have provided many constructive comments and suggestions, they were not asked to endorse the conclusions or recommendations nor did they see the final draft of the report before its release. The review of this report was overseen by Ulric Neisser, Department of Psychology, Cornell University. Appointed by the National Research Council, he was responsible for making certain that an independent examination of this report was carried out in accordance with institutional procedures and that all review comments were carefully considered. Responsibility for the final content of this report rests entirely with the authoring committee and the institution.

Many individuals deserve recognition for their contributions to the workshop and this report. Joah Iannotta served as the research assistant for this project, contributing to the development of the agenda and identification of speakers; she also contributed substantively to the content and structure of the report. Mary Graham, associate director for dissemination and communication of the Board on Children, Youth, and Families, provided feedback on numerous drafts and helped improve the clarity and readability of the report. In the Division on Behavioral and Social Sciences and Education, Christine McShane's editing skills provided the polish to complete the report and ensured that the report traversed all the right steps toward publication. Committee members Sandra Calvert and Robin Raskin devoted extra time at committee meetings to provide extremely thoughtful critiques of the report. Sandra and Robin's comments along with those of Jane Ross, director of the Center for Social and Economic Studies, significantly improved the quality of the report. We thank them for their efforts.

Michele D. Kipke, Director
Board on Children, Youth, and Families

Herbert Lin, Senior Scientist
Computer Science and Telecommunications Board

1

Introduction

The Internet plays an increasingly important role in the lives of children and adults as a vast repository of information, a source of entertainment, and a platform for new means of communication. Conservative estimates suggest that, on average, Internet traffic has doubled every year during the past decade, and estimates of the number of Internet hosts have risen from 1 million in 1992 to 10 million in 1996 (Odlyzko, 2000; Public Broadcasting Service, no date). These figures represent increases in both the number of individuals accessing the Internet as well as significant increases in the amount of content viewed by users. In addition to supplying more individuals with more online content, the Internet has stimulated new ways of sharing and compiling information that have notable implications for users. For example, chat rooms dedicated to supporting individuals struggling with cancer allow people in disparate locations to share encouragement as well as recent developments in cancer research (see <www.sharedexperience.org>).[1] New advances in human-computer interaction have improved rates of on-time immunization of children, made possible new approaches to improving nutrition education and health promotion, and even screened users for HIV through interview-based methodologies (Alemi et al., 1996; Kraak and Pelletier, 1998; Locke et al., 1992).

---

[1]A list of web sites mentioned in the text is included in the References section of the report.

Young people account for a significant proportion of Internet users and are the first generation to grow up digital—many of them do not remember what life was like before the Internet. Children have access to the Internet in an ever-increasing number of settings, including schools, libraries, homes, community centers, and commercial Internet cafés. This growing access means that young people have at their fingertips a wealth of educational content that schools and public libraries of previous generations could never offer. Indeed, while a library's collection of books and journals may be limited by its budget and space, a computer terminal and a phone line place the entirety of the Internet at hand. Today's students can create multimedia school reports, express their thoughts by publishing their own web pages online, and communicate with peers living in other countries. Clearly, such ready access to information is a boon to anyone invested in improving education and empowering individuals through knowledge.

The Internet is not, however, without problems or controversies. The same qualities that make it a beneficial tool—fast access to information; a venue for a free exchange of ideas among individuals in a variety of geographic locations, with different life experiences and values; and the opportunity for anyone to publish content online—are also problematic. As the amount of information online grows, the skills required to find educational content on the Internet become increasingly complex (Keller et al., 2001). At the same time, the possibility that young people will encounter content that is misleading or perhaps inappropriate for their age and maturity is a growing concern for many educators, librarians, parents, and other people responsible for overseeing children's Internet use.

Public concern that young people may encounter sexually explicit and other inappropriate material online has been coupled with increased interest in the availability of developmentally appropriate tools and strategies, both technological and nontechnical, that can protect children from online content that they may not have the resources to handle. At the request of Congress, the Computer Science and Telecommunications Board, jointly with the Board on Children, Youth, and Families of the National Research Council and the Institute of Medicine, formed the Committee on the Study of Tools and Strategies for Protecting Children from Pornography on the Internet and Their Applicability to Other Inappropriate Internet Content. This committee was charged with the task of exploring the pros and cons of different technology options and operational policies as well as nontechnical approaches that could facilitate young people's positive Internet use and experience. As a part of the committee's work, it convened a workshop

INTRODUCTION 3

focused on nontechnical strategies and brought together an interdisciplinary group of researchers, educators, policy makers, practitioners, and other key stakeholders to consider how to create effective strategies to protect children from pornography and other inappropriate material on the Internet that do not rely on technical tools.

QUESTIONS ADDRESSED BY THE WORKSHOP

The workshop focused on four key questions:

1. What is known about how young people (including young children as well as adolescents) use the Internet, and, from a child development perspective, what does existing research say about the impact of exposure to sexually explicit and other harmful material?
2. What framework does this knowledge offer for designing effective and age-appropriate nontechnical strategies?
3. What strategies of this type have been used in schools, libraries, and at home?
4. What further research is needed, and what opportunities exist to bridge research, policy, and practice to improve children's online experiences?

Through presentations and panel discussions, workshop participants addressed these questions. Research and data from media studies and child development were reviewed, and practitioners from schools, libraries, and organizations that offer outreach and Internet education for parents discussed the nontechnical strategies that have been effective for them. Presenters also offered carefully considered thoughts on what factors need to be weighed and balanced in creating approaches for protecting children, including the potential harm from exposure to various types of inappropriate material for different age groups, the types of online activities children pursue and the proportion of time they spend using the Internet, and the concerns and opportunities posed by increasing access to the Internet in a variety of venues.

ISSUES AND CHALLENGES

It is important to note at the outset of this report that children's exposure to sexually explicit and other inappropriate content represents a highly contentious and complicated set of issues. Defining what constitutes inappropriate and sexually explicit content is in itself problematic. Communities and families have a wide variety of sensibilities about what categories of Internet content warrant attention (e.g., sexually explicit material, content that promotes violence or offers advice on constructing bombs or weapons, commercial marketing to young Internet users). They may also define these categories very differently (e.g., some parents might define nudity as inappropriate sexually explicit material while others might define it as hardcore pornography).

In addition to varying public perceptions and concerns about what Internet content may be problematic for young people is the fact that children's cognitive, emotional, and social development changes rapidly, from the time they may first look at a monitor as young children to late adolescence, when computers may be a daily part of their lives (National Research Council and Institute of Medicine, 2000). Because children's developmental needs change so greatly, content that may be inappropriate at an earlier age may or may not be inappropriate when children are older.

Very little empirical research exists to inform the public on the impact of sexually explicit and other inappropriate content on young people. It is therefore impossible to make definitive statements based on scientific research that sexually explicit or other types of content do or do not have harmful effects on young people. Thus, communities must rely on their own sensibilities in determining how best to approach this issue. What science can offer—as highlighted in this report—is a conceptual framework and a set of nontechnical strategies that may help communities and parents choose an approach that fits their values, concerns, and the needs of their children.

ORGANIZATION OF THE REPORT

This summary highlights key themes that emerged from the workshop discussions, including both issues on which views converged as well as points of contention. Following this introduction, Chapter 2 discusses key contextual issues and challenges that policy makers, local administrators (e.g., school principals, superintendents), and parents face in choosing an approach to reducing children's exposure to inappropriate online content. Chapter 3 reviews three areas of research that provide a scientific basis to developing age-appropriate, nontechnical strategies as well as a guide for adults in selecting an approach that matches the maturity, Internet use

INTRODUCTION 5

patterns, and needs of the young people they supervise. This research includes information on children's cognitive, social, emotional, and moral development; research on what we know (and do not know) about the impact of the media on young people; and recent empirical studies of children's media use. Chapter 4 presents a wide variety of nontechnical strategies, describing these approaches and how communities might make use of them. Chapter 5 summarizes workshop participants' ideas for how to improve and connect future research, policy, and practice. The final chapter summarizes key points and areas emphasized by workshop participants.

This report reflects some of the key issues in the workshop and offers a first step in creating resources that will help communities develop comprehensive and carefully chosen nontechnical approaches to protecting children on the Internet. It is not, however, intended as a comprehensive review of the literature in any of the fields represented, nor do the examples of nontechnical strategies offer a complete or exhaustive list of available options. In addition, not all of the strategies discussed would necessarily be effective across all settings (e.g., home use versus access in an Internet café) or with all age groups. The strategies presented, however, were effective for the particular communities in which the speakers worked and thus offer a useful point of departure for communities and individuals seeking to develop their own approaches. Both the Board on Children, Youth, and Families and the Computer Science and Telecommunications Board hope that the workshop and this report will serve as a stimulus and resource for those who are charged with facilitating young people's Internet experience.

2

The Context of Strategy Development: The Needs of Schools and Parents

In his opening remarks, Committee Chair Richard Thornburgh told participants that the workshop focused on nontechnical strategies in part because "technology-based protections can never be entirely perfect or even reliable . . . so it is necessary to look at social mechanisms to help protect kids." Good policy can help promote appropriate solutions tailored to individual and community needs, Thornburgh said. Designing an effective approach to protecting children requires awareness of the particular issues and challenges confronting policy in this area.

This chapter describes some of the key contextual challenges that parents, teachers, and policy makers face in designing an approach to reducing children's exposure to inappropriate material Internet content. It begins with the workshop participants' definitions of "young people," "inappropriate material," and "nontechnical strategies." Next it reviews some of the ways in which young people can come in contact with sexually explicit or other inappropriate material. Many of these are not readily apparent and pose a particular set of challenges that need to be considered in formulating a response. Finally, this chapter describes children's educational needs and parents' concerns as they pertain to the Internet. These represent two critical aspects of the social context that may influence the formulation of responses to this topic, and workshop participants offered views on how to address these needs.

DEFINITIONS

In order to offer useful information to educators, parents, and others supervising children's Internet activities, the workshop talked broadly about the needs of young people and explored strategies that covered a wide age range, from the youngest ages through the end of adolescence. Computer technology and the Internet can enter a child's life very early—babies and toddlers may sit on a parent's lap to play with software oriented to their age, middle school children are now being assigned Internet research projects, and high school students routinely use the Internet. Communities also have varying beliefs about the age through which young people should be protected from inappropriate material.

As noted in the introduction, "inappropriate material" is not easily defined in great part because families, communities, and cultures have very different concepts about what constitutes inappropriate material. For example, in the current U.S. social context, particular concern has centered on children's exposure to pornography and material that may be classified as obscene. In many European countries, however, young people's exposure to graphic violence or hate speech is of greater concern, and sexually explicit material is not perceived to be of significant consequence.

In general, when the term "inappropriate material" is used in this report, it indicates a broad range of material from which communities might wish to shield their children. Workshop participants used "inappropriate material" to include Internet content that is sexually explicit or violent, hate speech such as Nazi and Holocaust-denial sites, material that could encourage young people to engage in illegal or risky behavior (e.g., directions for making bombs, purchasing guns, or pro-drug, alcohol, or tobacco sites), commercial ventures that target children for direct marketing campaigns, and web sites that violate young people's privacy by encouraging them to disclose personal information (e.g., address, home phone number, social security number, parent's credit card).

"Inappropriate material" also may refer to inappropriate contact between an Internet user and a young person. For instance, a young person could receive a sexually explicit instant message from another individual seeking to foster an online relationship that could lead to a face-to-face meeting. An online message represents another way young people can come in contact with inappropriate material, while a face-to-face meeting, if the young person agrees to it, has more serious implications for children's physical safety. Parents want to protect their children, and the online safety of young people represents an important aspect of the workshop discussions.

During the workshop, participants worked to develop an operational definition of what constitutes "nontechnical strategies." This proved challenging because no clear line differentiates technical tools from nontechnical strategies, and many examples emerged that incorporate both technical and nontechnical approaches. For example, a teacher who designs a home page with links to web sites she determines are relevant to a lesson uses both technical skills (e.g., creating the web page) as well as nontechnical methods (e.g., making decisions about what content to limit her students to viewing during the lesson).

In general, nontechnical strategies are those focused on training individuals to use the Internet effectively and safely, that increase online skills to reduce exposure to inappropriate content, or that make individual users more resistant to messages implicit in inappropriate content. For instance, establishing a code of acceptable Internet use and online behavior can help to ensure that young people use the Internet safely and wisely. Strategies such as media literacy teach critical thinking skills that may serve to make individual users more resistant to messages implicit in inappropriate content (Singer and Singer, 1993). Finally, curricula that improve users' skills with search engines and web browsing as well as the development of beneficial, educational web content may help to reduce exposure to inappropriate content. In contrast, technical tools are designed by creating new hardware and software meant to reduce young people's exposure to inappropriate material. Technical tools assign the task of screening inappropriate content to computers and software, whereas nontechnical strategies make individuals personally responsible for decisions about what content will be viewed.

COMING IN CONTACT WITH INAPPROPRIATE CONTENT

Surfing the Internet and accidentally or intentionally viewing web sites that contain inappropriate content are how many people imagine their children may be exposed to material they may find objectionable. Because the Internet is not just a repository of information that may be passively browsed, but rather a dynamic and interactive system, the opportunity for users to be exposed to inappropriate content is not limited to viewing web sites alone. For example, chat room "talk" can become its own form of sexually explicit material, bulletin boards or newsgroups may contain graphic language or may center on inappropriate themes, Internet users are sometimes "spammed" with emails that link to pornographic images, and individual users can be contacted directly through instant messaging or email by online predators or market research that may encourage young people to disclose personal information.

Speakers were concerned about these interactive platforms through which young people could encounter inappropriate material, some participants noting that these interactive formats (e.g., in chat rooms or through offensive material posted by a student about a classmate) could be potentially more harmful than passively surfing web sites. The participatory nature of these formats raises concerns. As noted by Patricia Greenfield, professor of psychology at the University of California, Los Angeles, young people participating in these formats can engage in behavior that violates conventional normative standards of social conduct. They can also be encouraged to meet face-to-face with other users if they are contacted directly, putting them in potential physical danger. Presenters encouraged the development of strategies that would not only reduce young people's exposure to inappropriate web sites but would also teach online safety that could help protect them from unsafe or upsetting interactions with other users.

SOCIAL CONTEXT:
CHALLENGES IN DEVELOPING AN APPROACH

Policy makers, parents, teachers, school administers, librarians, and other adults charged with the task of facilitating young people's Internet use face a number of challenges in designing an approach to dealing with inappropriate Internet content. Initial challenges include defining inappropriate content—a particular challenge for organizations that serve the community—and remaining aware of the many ways in which young people can come in contact with inappropriate material.

The following section reflects the discussions of the workshop's two keynote speakers—Linda Roberts, director of the Office of Educational Technology and senior adviser to the Secretary of the U.S. Department of Education, and Anne Thompson, program commissioner of the National Parent Teacher Association. Roberts discussed the school landscape as it has been shaped by federal policy to stimulate the development of technology in the schools, how protecting children from inappropriate material fits into the larger mission of the educational system, and the potential impact that filtering and blocking software can have on adult supervision of children's online activities. Thompson focused her discussion on parents, noting three areas that make reducing children's contact with inappropriate online content more challenging: lack of parental awareness around this issue, the broad range of parental attitudes toward the Internet, and parents' lack of technical proficiency.

School Context and Children's Educational Needs

Linda Roberts identified the Clinton administration's goals for improving technology resources in schools as "computers, connection, teachers, and content." The department's highest priority was to get computers into schools and to "get schools wired" (i.e., connected to the Internet). Substantial differences exist in the extent to which school districts have computers in labs and classrooms, and even more variation in the extent to which these computers are connected to the Internet. Increasing the number of computers in schools as well as encouraging the penetration of high-speed connections to the Internet in underserved areas had been the highest priority for the Clinton administration, Roberts said. See Box 2-1 for additional information on what is called the digital divide.

The Department of Education's second priority has been to create new opportunities for training teachers in effective use of technology and incorporating it into their course work and curricula. Knowledgeable facilitators can make the difference between using computers for simple drilling and teaching young people to use software to express their ideas, seek information, and integrate knowledge. Finally, the department recognized the great need for software and online resources that are challenging, stimulating, and informative. These tools are important in developing useful educational content and creating an enriching technology landscape for students.

For Roberts, children's access to inappropriate material on the Internet represents one important thread within the larger context of educating young people to be competent, skillful, and savvy users of technology. She suggested that the issue needs to be considered carefully with four points in mind. First, because every student needs access to resources that engage them in learning and refining skills and therefore must be connected to the Internet, schools need to be concerned that high-quality and reliable content is available on the web. Students need to have fast access to useful material, and class time is wasted if students have to spend considerable time sifting through irrelevant content to get at the resources they need.

Second, the developmental needs of children must be carefully taken into consideration in determining what material is appropriate at what age.

BOX 2-1
dig·i·tal di·vide

As society moves from the industrial to the information age, technological skill and fluency are essential in an increasingly competitive and global economy, and technical savvy may stand to create the next significant gap in wages between those who possess technical skills and those who do not. A growing digital divide has already been observed with racial minorities and individuals in low socioeconomic classes having far less access to computer technology, the Internet, and high-speed connections.

A study by the Kaiser Family Foundation showed that while 78 percent of white children had computers in their homes, only 55 percent of black children and 48 percent of Hispanic children had a home computer. White children were also more likely to have Internet access in the home—54 percent had Internet access compared with 29 percent of black children or 24 percent of Hispanic children (Roberts et al., 1999). In addition, when it comes to having high-quality technology in the home—defined as computer technology that includes a hard drive, CD-ROM, printer, modem or Internet access, and a mouse or other pointer control device—this disparity is again replicated (Becker, 2000). Only 10 percent of black and 13 percent of Hispanic children are likely to have access to this level of technology at home (Becker, 2000).

The socioeconomic status (SES) of parents is also a significant influence on children's access to computers and the Internet at home and school. For example, as community income levels rise, so does the availability of computers and access to the Internet in children's homes. In communities with median incomes under $25,000, computer and Internet access for whites and blacks is 49 and 23 percent, respectively, while the same access for children in homes with median incomes over $40,000 is 81 and 58 percent, respectively (Roberts et al., 1999).

More importantly, however, SES has been linked to a second type of digital divide that goes beyond access to the types of skills that are acquired. SES influences the way in which technology is taught to and used by children in schools. One study finds that, "although low-SES schools are beginning to catch up to high-SES schools in some benchmarks of access, the more sophisticated and creative uses of computers are not yet well linked with the curricula in core academic subjects, especially in poorer schools" (Becker, 2000, p. 56). In other words, children in low-SES schools are more likely to use computers for drill-and-practice rather than to

continues

> *continued*
>
> communicate ideas, search for information, or in a manner that requires the integration of skills and knowledge sets.
>
> These disparities are of great concern, given the fact that racial and ethnic minority children comprise a disproportionate share of those with low-SES parents and of those residing in low-SES communities. Minorities are becoming an increasing share of the nation's students and workers, and its economic stability and vitality may rest with its ability to fashion systematic means to provide equality of access, use, and quality of technology among all segments of the population (Novak and Hoffman, 1998).

"It's not a simple matter to do the right thing," Roberts stated, alluding to the inherent difficulties in screening the vast amount of information on the Internet in addition to determining what constitutes inappropriate material and for what age groups. Schools have traditionally been concerned that children not only make academic progress, but also develop socially, cognitively, and emotionally. For technology as well, it is important for schools to create an environment in which students not only achieve the skills to be facile with technology, but also have their developmental needs fostered by the learning they do online. Successful nontechnical strategies are developed with children's developmental needs in mind.

Third, schools must also be concerned with online safety. As a part of this, educators must strive to create environments that prevent young people from getting onto paths that might be harmful to their development and ultimately to society. Hence, schools need to be concerned not only about sexually explicit material but also hate material, content that is untruthful or misleading, and online experiences that may draw children to sites that are not beneficial for them. Finally, schools need to prepare students for the information age by ensuring that they have literacy skills—basic literacy, information literacy, and media literacy—that help to ensure their future in a global economy. Not only do media and information literacy teach young people useful cognitive skills like effective search strategies, critical thinking, and learning to evaluate sources for reliability and validity, but also these same skills can help prevent children from stumbling onto inappropriate material in the first place or from being drawn in by misinformation and messages that run contrary to their values.

Technical tools, such as filtering and blocking software, are a growing part of both the school and home environments. At the time of the workshop, legislation that would make filtering mandatory for all schools was pending in Congress. Such technical tools may be compatible with non-technical strategies, although one's individual views may make filtering an acceptable or objectionable response. Nonetheless, both Roberts and Thompson identified two very important concerns that tend to be overlooked during heated First Amendment debates that take place when filtering is discussed.

Filters tend to create a sense of safety among parents, teachers, and schools, and this often allows teachers to spend more time on instruction and less time policing student's online activities or in the office discussing this issue with parents. The risk is that parents and teachers may become complacent about young people's exposure to questionable material online. If schools and parents rely exclusively on filtering, they may not prepare students for the inevitable instances of failure to screen objectionable material and may not have a plan for addressing exposure if it does occur. In addition, young people will eventually have unrestricted access to the web, and conveying ethical perspectives on the use of the Internet is a valuable message that may be neglected if filters are not recognized as imperfect.

Parental Awareness and Involvement

Thompson detailed several challenges to helping parents in trying to protect their children from inappropriate material on the Internet. The first challenge is increasing their awareness of the risks of children's Internet use in a way similar to other issues of public health and safety. Many parents are not yet aware of the extent to which their children could come in contact with pornography—intentionally or unintentionally—while surfing online, nor are they aware of some of the dangers inherent in online venues like chat rooms. This lack of awareness means that parents cannot effectively caution their children about how to be safe online. Few parents fail to warn their children about the dangers of talking to a stranger in the park or revealing personal information like their home address. Many, however, do not caution their children about disclosing such information online. The results of a child's disclosing personal information online could be mild, if it is to an online business, for example—a parent might notice a slight increase in junk mail or junk email—or the consequences could be much more serious. Thompson stressed the importance of making parents more aware of Internet safety and that they cannot abdicate this responsibility to filters, schools, or libraries.

Attitudes toward the Internet pose another challenge. Despite the availability of sexually explicit material, most parents agree that the Internet is an extremely useful and productive tool in improving academic performance and preparing their children for a technology-driven society. As a result, few parents would cancel Internet services to prevent access to pornography. However, there is a broad range of attitudes among parents about whether or not to restrict their children's Internet use, whether to monitor their activities online, and how to do so (National School Boards Association, no date). Box 2-2 describes several recent studies that attempt to assess parents' and children's attitudes toward the Internet. Parents may

---

BOX 2-2
Parents' and Children's Attitudes Toward the Internet

Several recent studies have attempted to capture parents' and children's attitudes toward the Internet.

Internet Attitudes

A study by the National School Boards Association indicated that children and parents overall see the Internet as a very valuable tool. Data suggested that the Internet is influencing how students learn and that it may be improving children's attitude about learning. In this survey, 43 percent of 9- to 17-year-olds stated that the Internet has improved their attitude toward school, and 17 percent stated that the Internet has improved their attitude a lot. Parents are even more positive about the Internet, viewing it as a powerful tool for learning and communicating, citing a desire to connect their children to the Internet to benefit their education as the primary reason for buying a home computer and purchasing Internet service.

Parents are concerned, however, about Internet security, privacy, and the potential for their children to access inappropriate material. In a study by Penn et al. (2000), half of parents were very concerned both that their children might access web sites that are not appropriate for them and that children might make inappropriate contact with a stranger online. In all, 39 percent of parents were very concerned that children might give out personal information; 32 percent were concerned that their children might play violent or inappropriate games online; and 21 percent were very concerned that children might give out a credit card number to another online user who should not have access to it.

Limiting Internet Access

Although parents in one survey expressed concern about some of the content their children might be exposed to as well as some of the interactions their children might have, 41 percent of teens in this survey stated that their parents have not provided rules to regulate their Internet activity. In a survey by *FamilyPC* Magazine, many teens reported that their parents have used strategies to limit their Internet access. More than half of teens (54 percent) stated that their parents check on them when they are online; 43 percent stated that parents have strict rules about where they can (and cannot) go online; and 42 percent of teens reported that the computer is kept in a room where it can be observed (Survey on teen use of technology, 2000). Interestingly, only 15 percent of teens stated that their parents use blocking features on their Internet service providers, and only 6 percent said that their parents bought and installed blocking software.

Gaps Between Parents and Children

Penn et al. (2000) found that the Internet has become another arena in which parents attempt to stay aware of their children's activities and young people attempt to evade their oversight. Several gaps exist in what parents perceive and what young people are actually doing. For instance, 45 percent of teens say they have personal online profiles, but only 17 percent of parents thought their teens had such profiles. 81 percent of teens say they have private email accounts, while only 68 percent of parents thought their teens had these accounts. More than half of the teens reported corresponding with strangers, and only 30 percent of parents thought their teens sent or received email from a stranger.

The National School Boards Association report uncovered a gap between parents and children about how much supervision children actually receive online: 67 percent of parents report that someone else is in the room while their children are online, while 78 percent of 13- to 17-year-olds say they use the Internet when they are alone. In addition, parents routinely overstate the extent to which their children use the Internet for educational purposes and underestimate the extent to which their children use the Internet for entertainment. For example, 76 percent of parents whose children log on at home say their children use the Internet for schoolwork at least once a week; 63 percent of teenagers agreed with this statement.

struggle with concerns about invading their children's privacy, and these concerns may encourage them to adopt a hands-off approach to the Internet. Trust in a child's decision-making capabilities is best offered when both parents and children are aware of the risks and clear guidelines exist for acceptable Internet use.

Finally, even if parents know the extent to which they want to restrict or monitor their children's use, many are unsure of how to follow through because they lack technical proficiency. Some parents are unsure about using technical tools and may assume (sometimes rightly) that their children may know better than they how to disable a filter or erase temporary log files. Similarly, parents are also frequently unaware of nontechnical strategies that could be helpful in establishing boundaries, defining appropriate behavior online, and developing consequences if their children do not follow the rules. Thompson stated that parents are in great need of strategies that are simple, clear, readily available, easy to use, and that help support them in setting limits for online activity. Educating children about the Internet and how to avoid material parents view as inappropriate should become as routine a part of parenting as teaching a child to cross the street safely.

3

Creating a Framework for Developing Effective Nontechnical Strategies

The second part of the workshop was devoted an exploration of what is known about the potential impact of sexually explicit material on children; the social, emotional, and moral developmental needs of young people; and data on how young people use the Internet. Research on these questions can help in making decisions about where and how to spend resources and set priorities about preventing children's exposure to various types of material.

This chapter is divided into three sections. The first discusses research that has attempted identify what impact or effects the media may have on children. As noted earlier in this report, the number of empirical studies on the impact of sexually explicit material is extremely limited, and researchers are very cautious about the conclusions that can be drawn from existing studies. The second section reviews material on children's social, emotional, and moral development in light of what it suggests for creating effective nontechnical strategies and improving the quality of kids' online experiences. Finally, this chapter discusses children's Internet use—for what purposes children go online and the extent to which the Internet is or is not a significant part of their lives.

RESEARCH ON THE MEDIA

Research on the impact of sexually explicit material on children is limited, primarily due to ethical considerations of conducting the types of experiments that would clearly demonstrate what consequences exposure has or does not have on young people. For example, a study design in which children were shown sexually explicit material in order to identify short- and long-term effects of exposure would be unacceptable: it would be unethical to expose them to material thought potentially to have a negative impact in order to measure and identify this impact. However, as this chapter discusses, researchers have been able to conduct some clinical studies using media content other than sexually explicit content—research on violent material is one such example. This is because our society has more permissive attitudes about allowing young people to view violent material compared with sexually explicit material. In addition, a few studies of sexually explicit material have used college-age viewers as a way of extrapolating the impact this material may have on younger populations (Donnerstein and Linz, 1986; Zillmann, 1982; Zillmann and Bryant, 1982; Zillmann and Weaver, 1999).

Workshop participants extrapolated cautiously from empirical studies on violent media content to sexually explicit material, since similar learning processes underlie how exposure may lead to impact. They discussed research on sexually violent material done with college-age students as well as research that examines what effects sexuality in the media may have on adolescents. This research does not deal with pornography, but rather the type of sexually laden themes one finds in soap operas and women's magazines. These are media forms that many young people are exposed to, although they do not contain the type of explicit sexuality one finds in adult movies or magazines.

Violent Material

According to Joanne Cantor, professor at the University of Wisconsin, Madison, several types of effects have been observed in studies of violent media content and children: desensitization, increases in hostility, imitation and disinhibition, and fear and anxiety responses. Desensitization occurs when an emotional response to a stimulus is diminished after repeated exposure to that stimulus. This can be adaptive—a doctor who becomes accustomed to seeing blood and does not have the strong emotional response he experienced in medical school is of benefit to his patients. The media, however, creates fantasy exposures to content that can cause arousal and, over time, desensitization when it is not necessarily (and often not) adaptive. For example, a child who sees a graphic, violent image might become angry or frightened. If this image is a representation and not an actual event, then the typical reactions of "fight or flight" are not appropriate or functional. With repeated exposure, a child may cease to have these emotional responses (Calvert, 1999; Cantor, 2000). Research has shown that desensitization to media violence can result in reduced arousal and emotional disturbance while witnessing actual violence, greater hesitancy to call an adult to intervene in a witnessed physical altercation, and less sympathy for victims of abuse and assault (Cline et al., 1973; Molitor and Hirsch, 1994; Mullin and Linz, 1995).

Increases in hostility after watching violent content in the media have also been observed. In one study, college students who watched violent films for four days were more likely, when given the opportunity, to interfere with another individual's future employment chances (Zillman and Weaver, 1999). Repeat viewing of violent material seemed to create an enduring hostile mental framework that discouraged viewers from interacting positively with others, even those who had not provoked them. Cantor also cited a study in Israeli middle schools after the introduction of the World Wrestling Federation to Israeli television. This study documented the widespread imitation of acts demonstrated on this show that resulted in an epidemic of playground injuries (Lemish, 1997). Social learning theory suggests that children learn through observation and modeling of behaviors and actions, and it is often used to explain the phenomenon of children imitating what they see on television or in films.

Young people of a wide range of ages sometimes experience fear and anxiety as a result of exposure to television (Owens et al., 1999; Singer et al., 1998). Results can range from nightmares and temporary sleep disturbances to more lasting effects, such as a fear of swimming in the ocean after watching the movie *Jaws* (Harrison and Cantor, 1999). Which specific types of content are likely to cause fear will depend on the child's developmental level. As examples, preschool-age children are most disturbed by grotesque, visual images such as monsters, whereas children in elementary school may be more likely to be frightened by realistic images in which the danger they perceive could actually happen. Teenagers tend to be more frightened by abstract components of a story. Data that Cantor collected during the Persian Gulf conflict showed that elementary school children became frightened by images of exploding missiles, whereas teen viewers were more afraid of the idea that the conflict could spread. Material frightening to a teenager may not even be processed by a younger child, who may not understand the abstract concepts that are less readily visualized (Cantor, 1998; Cantor et al., 1993).

Responses to media violence can be cumulative (e.g., attitudinal changes from repeat exposure) or instantaneous (e.g., fear responses due to seeing the "wrong" movie at the "wrong" developmental moment), and they may be temporary or lasting (e.g., a few nightmares or a lasting fear of specific animals or situations). Cantor cautioned that more research is needed before extrapolating results from this research on violent material to sexually explicit media content. She was, however, more confident about extrapolating from research on violence to sexually violent material.

Sexually Violent Material

Ed Donnerstein, dean and professor of communication at the University of California, Santa Barbara, discussed research on the effects of viewing sexually violent images on college-age viewers, noting that effects were observed in these studies similar to effects in studies of violence alone. Studies of young adults (ages 18-20) watching an hour of the equivalent of an R-rated film containing sexual violence demonstrate desensitization immediately following this viewing. Arousal levels decrease with additional viewing after the first hour. Furthermore, viewers who are shown a documentary on battered women after one hour of a sexually violent film demonstrate less empathy toward the victims, and lower evaluations of how injured the woman was and how painful the experience may have been. Attitudinal changes are also observed, with both men and women more likely to display callous attitudes toward female victims, such as stating that a rape was the fault of the victim or that she brought it on herself (Donnerstein and Linz, 1986; Zillman, 1982; Zillmann and Bryant, 1982). According to Donnerstein, women viewers do have slightly different responses from men, and although both show desensitization, women also tend to experience an increase in fear after watching sexually violent content (Krafka et al., 1997).

Although changes in attitude and arousal levels were measured in these studies, Donnerstein noted that it is not clear the extent to which these changes may be lasting. For example, normal arousal responses tend to return after 24 hours, and the "long-term" changes in attitudes are based on studies that follow subjects for only a few weeks after viewing films. Interestingly, studies of young adults exposed to sexually explicit content that was not violent did not demonstrate that desensitization occurred (Linz et al., 1988, 1989).

Donnerstein also stated that research has never demonstrated that viewing sexually explicit or sexually violent content results in viewers' committing sexually violent crimes or behaviors. Zillmann's arousal theory offers some insight as to why sexually explicit content would not lead to any specific or consistent behavioral outcome in a group of viewers. Although sexually explicit content may produce emotional or physiological arousal, behavioral outcomes could result in sexual expression, aggressive behavior, or altruism. The outcome will depend on the personality of the viewer, the environment, and context in which the material was viewed (Huston et al., 1998).

Sexuality and Sexually Laden Material

While Cantor and Donnerstein focused on media that was violent and sexually violent, Jane Brown, professor of journalism and mass communication at the University of North Carolina, centered her remarks on sexuality in the media, asking: What do we know about how teens learn about sexuality from the media? Her presentation reflected both theory and research. For example, uses and gratification theory suggests that the potential impact of sexual content is tied to what motivates young people to view media content (Huston et al., 1998). Similarly, cognitive developmental theory suggests that how young people interpret media content is dependent on their developmental level (Huston et al., 1998). Research on the impact of sexually explicit content must therefore be understood in the context of why young people choose media content and what may drive their interpretation of this content.

According to Brown, adolescents are very interested in sexuality and beginning in early adolescence go through a normative developmental process in which they begin to look for information on sex and their bodies as they begin to develop a sexual self. Adolescents often turn to the media for information on sexuality for several reasons, including to seek information they cannot obtain from parents or schools and to find specific answers to questions that are embarrassing to ask (Brown and Stern, in press). Brown described the types of information adolescents may be seeking in the media, the benefits and problems they face in getting information from the media, and research that identifies potential areas of impact of sexuality and sexually explicit material in the media.

Although most would agree that it would be ideal for young people to seek out their parents for information on sexuality, parents are still reluctant to talk to their children about sex. The information parents do tend to provide is about physical development and the bodily changes young people experience as well as a discussion about abstinence. While it is important for parents to convey to their children the personal values they hold about when and how to choose to be sexually active, many parents talk to their children about abstinence and nothing else.

In addition, because it is often difficult for parents to talk about passion and desire with their children, young people sometimes find it difficult to "buy into" a clinical discussion (Brown et al., 1990; Strasburger, 1989; Strouse and Fabes, 1985). Considering that young people are often surrounded by images of sexuality that are completely centered around desire, it is not hard to understand why parents and children often do not communicate effectively about sex. Adolescents are therefore left with many unanswered questions, and they often turn to their friends—who often have much *mis*information to share—as well as to the media (Sutton et al., 2001).

Many schools are also not providing the type of comprehensive sex education classes that they have in the past. For example, the state of North Carolina has stipulated that only abstinence may be discussed in sex education classes. This means that young people seeking information about contraception need to find another source. Brown stated that if parents and schools are not providing young people with answers to questions that go beyond abstinence, many young people will turn elsewhere to get additional information about sexuality.

The media can fill this gap, providing information that parents and schools are not discussing and providing a comfortable venue for young people to seek information. Brown stated the media often make young people more comfortable in seeking information in that it is accessible, anonymous, doesn't talk back (unless you are in a chat room), and is less embarrassing than most of other sexual socialization sources. Adolescents can find not only specific information on such things as contraception and sexually transmitted diseases, but also an arena for resolving questions such as, "Am I normal? Is my body normal? Am I developing appropriately at the right speed? What is a tampon and how do I use it? How do you date? How do you kiss?" All of which is, Brown reminded participants, "for teens, very embarrassing stuff."

In addition to trying to find out if their bodies are developing normally, teens also begin to have questions about relationships and how to initiate sexual contact. Brown referred to this set of questions as pertaining to the development of "relationship scripts" or schemas, meaning that young people can use the media to establish socially normative behavior patterns for sexuality (Huston et al., 1998, p. 13). For example, teens may look for answers that will tell them how to behave normally when they are dating, kissing, and even how to act after a kiss—can you just return to a conversation? Television and movies in particular, and to some extent print media, can provide information about these issues by depicting scenes in which these activities take place, and teens can watch to see how other people resolve these situations (Pardun, 2001).

That young people often turn to the media to sort out some of these issues is both positive and negative. On one hand, many young people may find reassurance that their curiosity about sexuality and the changes in their bodies are normal and they need not feel ashamed of their changing physiques and changing interests. On the other hand, using the media as a resource can be problematic. For example, bodies portrayed in the media as sexually attractive are often unattainable (e.g., very thin physiques for girls and well-defined, sizable muscles for boys), and a young person who perceives his or her body as not fitting into these norms may be troubled rather than reassured (Heinberg and Thompson, 1995; Hofschire and Greenberg, 2001).

Although some literature exists on traditional forms of media (e.g., television, radio, magazines), the number of empirical studies are extremely limited. For instance, in a Kaiser Family Foundation report reviewing existing research on the media, Huston, Wartella, and Donnerstein (1998) found no more than 15 empirical studies on this topic. In addition, research on how young people use the Internet to learn about sexuality is in its infancy.

Research on print media suggests that turning to the media for information on sexuality is a normative behavior among teens. The majority of adolescent boys have seen at least one issue of *Playboy*, while girls tend to turn to women's magazines—for example, *Seventeen Magazine* for young teens and, for girls older than 14, *Glamour* and *Cosmopolitan*. Magazines like *Glamour* provide very explicit information on topics such as relationships with boys and content devoted to sex, flirting, and various romantic aspects of relationships. Brown described this content as depicting sexuality as recreation, competition, and a commodity in which men and masculinity often represent power, women are portrayed as passive, and sex is depicted as a tool of femininity through which women might gain power.

These messages culminate in a narrative about gender and sexuality that Brown termed the romantic heterosexual script. The messages about sexuality contained in this script tend to be irresponsible and potentially emotionally and physically unhealthy, and this script is present in both the mainstream media and in pornography, although it tends to be more overt in the latter. Brown explained that the script itself is problematic in that it answers adolescent's questions about sexuality with messages that do not always represent safe or healthy choices. Pornography may "up the ante" in that the messages are very explicit and overt. However, research has not answered questions of the extent to which overt versus implicit messages like those in mainstream media have more impact on viewers.

Most studies of the impact of sexually explicit material in the media on adolescents' sexual attitudes and practices have been limited to the sexual content in mainstream media. These studies suggest that impact is shaped significantly by the specific messages contained in the content that is viewed (Huston et al., 1998). Although research in this area is extremely limited, studies have suggested that frequent television viewers tend to have more negative attitudes toward remaining a virgin and that becoming a nonvirgin is a priority (Brown and Newcomer, 1991; Strouse et al., 1995). These studies are correlational, however, so it is possible that a third factor, such as different values and beliefs about sexual activity, is actually responsible for this trend and television viewing is an extraneous variable.

Brown identified some of the significant messages in the media as suggesting to adolescents that they should be thinking about sexuality, that they should be thinking about it early, and, implicitly, that they should not remain a virgin for long. Counter messages exist but are not abundant. Frequent television viewers are also less likely to believe that marriages are happy or lasting, prompted perhaps by the depiction of married couples who are not happy, not having sex, or are having sex with a person other than their spouse (Signorielli, 1991). Adolescents who watch soap operas frequently overestimate the extent to which it is easy to be a single mother and do not recognize the economic impact of single motherhood. Many of the characters depicted on television are wealthy and can hire nannies, continue their education, and may have significant leisure time (Larson, 1996). Music video viewing seems to increase the acceptance of premarital sex and interpersonal violence (Greenson and Williams, 1986; Kalof, 1999).

Many studies indicate that the media seems to have an effect on attitudes, although it is very difficult to assess whether these attitudes last well into the future, the extent to which these attitudes are related to behavior, and to what degree the media compared with other experiences in a young person's life are most influential in shaping the choices made. For example, although studies have shown that viewing fashion magazines tends to cause lower scores on body image indices in girls, not all girls develop anorexic behaviors.

Script and schema theories suggest that experience may be particularly important in determining the impact of sexual content in the media, and that individuals with less sexual experience may be more greatly affected than those who have less experience (Huston et al., 1998). In a study conducted by Brown in which early adolescent females were asked to keep journals about what they were observing in the media about love, sex, and relationships, the participants' experience was extremely important in shaping how they interpreted and reacted to sexuality in the media. One prepubertal 12-year-old who had not had sexual experiences did not want to see sex in the media and was upset by some of the depictions she observed. Older girls who were beginning to think about relationships were very interested in what can be called the romantic heterosexual script depicted in the media. Girls who had been sexually active were more critical of the media's portrayal of sexuality and the roles male and females should take (according to these representations). Experience, development, and age made enormous differences in the types of reactions girls had to the media.

Researchers have turned to cross-cultural studies in an effort to identify what type of connection may exist between exposure to sexually explicit material and behavioral outcomes, with limited success. Studies in which young people are exposed to nudity and explicit material at a relatively young age do not show higher levels of sexual addiction or teen pregnancy in European countries compared with the United States. However, European children also receive early, frequent, and comprehensive sexuality education in a way that is not typical in the United States. According to Brown, this could suggest that such education offers a useful context for interpreting sexually explicit material. It may also suggest that sexually explicit material does not have the type of impact on behavior that some may suspect.

Brown indicated some concerns about young people being surrounded by the explicit romantic heterosexual script through easy access to pornography on the Internet, but noted that the Internet is a powerful information tool for young people. For example, instead of turning to a scene from a movie for perspective on how couples handle intimacy, a young person could go to the American Social Health Association's teen sexual health web site <iwannaknow.org> and join a monitored chat room with other teens to talk anonymously about sexuality. Brown stated that the chat room supervised and facilitated by an expert in sexual health could be a more productive learning experience than the messages a young person may receive from a highly romanticized scene from a movie. She pointed out the very low number of web sites dedicated to sexual health and education compared with the large number of pages devoted to pornography available online. Brown urged that more resources should be devoted to developing more sexual health and "healthy sexuality" web sites to make it easier for adolescents to get absorbed in productive explorations about sexual health.

Summary of Research on the Media

The presentations on research on media impact converged on several points. The public develops many fears about new forms of media; this has been the true for the emergence of radio, television, and now the Internet (Wartella and Jennings, 2000). Despite these fears, the little research that has been conducted has not been able to establish definitively the impact of sexually explicit material on young people, nor have any causal relationships been identified between exposure to sexually explicit material in the media and behavioral outcomes. Studies on violent media content do consistently document desensitization, increases in hostility, imitation and disinhibition of aggressive responses, and fear and anxiety responses in participants. In young people, instantaneous responses (e.g., a one-time viewing) to violent media can sometimes result in fear and anxiety responses, such as nightmares. Studies in college-age populations suggest that repeated exposure to sexually violent media may encourage more callous attitudes about women. Research on adolescent female responses to sexual content in mainstream media suggests that their experience and developmental stage have a great influence on their interpretation of the media's portrayal of sexuality. Research on violence in the media has been more consistent in finding negative impact on subjects, while the more limited body of literature on nonviolent, sexually explicit material has had less consistent findings. Thus participants suggested that in terms of resource allocation, attention to sexually violent content on the Internet may represent a better priority than other nonviolent sexually explicit material. This panel also suggested the importance of parent interaction with young people about content online as well as the development of increased numbers of positive and engaging web sites for young people as a means to limit their exposure to material some parents may find objectionable.

SOCIAL, EMOTIONAL, AND MORAL DEVELOPMENT

The workshop provided an overview of the social, emotional, and moral development of children and adolescents as a framework for a more analytic perspective about how the Internet could influence development positively or negatively. Participants also explored what elements could create nontechnical strategies that not only may decrease young people's exposure to inappropriate online content, but also may make the Internet a more beneficial tool for them.

This section begins with an overview of children's social and emotional development, highlighting developmental milestones pertinent to structuring nontechnical strategies for young children through adolescence. Children's moral development is then considered, again tracking milestones for the youngest children who may be online through adolescence. Finally, the section examines how the Internet may affect and shape social norms for young people and what impact this may have.

Social and Emotional Development

Dorothy Singer, co-director of the Yale University Family Television Research and Consultation Center, reviewed the social and emotional developmental stages children go through and the insight these stages suggest about how technology may impact development. In a study Singer conducted for the Corporation for Public Broadcasting, children's computer proficiency was positively correlated with reading and math levels, interpersonal skills, cooperation, attentiveness, ability to follow directions, language skills, and imagination to computer proficiency (Singer and Singer, 1993). This study also found a negative correlation between computer proficiency and physical aggression, all of which suggest that computers and the Internet can be very beneficial as educational tools both in terms of cognition and social and emotional development.

In focusing on the stages of development and the types of technology that could benefit children's development, Singer echoed earlier statements about the need for web sites containing valid information matched to children's developmental interests and explorations about sexuality and sexual health, as a way to protect them from pornography. For example, children ages 3-5 are developing at a rapid rate and have many changing intellectual and social needs. This age group reasons intuitively rather than logically. They learn through action and senses and are concerned with why things happen rather than cause and effect. Preschoolers are learning to differentiate between external and internal events, are highly imaginative, believe wishes can influence reality, enjoy role playing and what-if games, and are developing a sense of humor that often centers on burlesque and slapstick. They are learning how to concentrate, associate words and symbols with objects, perceive and discriminate, identify similarity and difference, classify objects, recognize order and relationships, and develop concepts. This age group is curious, learning to explore and use creative imagination (Levine et al., 1983, pp. 97-107; National Research Council and Institute of Medicine, 2000, pp. 124-162).

Socially, 3-5-year-olds are beginning to see other children as individuals to be communicated with directly, although preschoolers tend to display self-centered forms of speech. They enjoy using words that shock their audience. Brief but frequent arguments break out in preschool groups, and play groups are flexible and easily disbanded. Preschoolers love dramatic play, can distinguish between fantasy and reality, although this is often challenging to them, and are becoming self-reliant (Levine et al., 1983, pp. 97-107; National Research Council and Institute of Medicine, 2000, pp. 163-181).

Preschoolers' emotional development is characterized by fluid and rapidly changing emotions ranging from independent to clingy, affectionate to hostile, secure to insecure. They are often jealous and have many fears, often about physical vulnerability, death, and loneliness. Thoughts and feelings are translated into words and actions immediately, often causing embarrassing moments for parents, who in turn encourage their children to think about what they are saying before they say or do it. Play—especially role playing and imaginative play—is extremely important in helping children to explore and test roles not yet possible in the real world (Levine et al., 1983, pp. 97-107; National Research Council and Institute of Medicine, 2000, pp. 105-115).

According to Singer, computer programs beneficial for this age group would be interactive and designed to engage children in activities parallel to those on screen. Such programs would take advantage of what-if games and encourage children to develop their own outcomes to a storyline or imaginary situation. Vivid and aesthetic depictions of the real world as well as fictional and fantastic would both appeal and stimulate this age group. Finally, long delays in cause-effect relationships in plots are to be avoided, and responses or consequences of action should be morally appropriate and fair.

While preschoolers are learning how to interact with other individuals, elementary schoolchildren (ages 6-9) are beginning to become aware of the social characteristics of the groups of which they are a part. They begin to see themselves in terms of their social roles and categories. Sex, age, race, religion, and class are meaningful concepts to this age group, and they are very curious about how these social roles make them similar and different from friends. This age group is often selective in choosing close friends, seeks lasting relationships, may make enemies, and does not shy from quarreling.

Six-to-nine-year-olds recognize that they are part of a subculture (e.g., their peer group) with values, rules, codes, language, superstition, and make-believe games, and this subculture is an important source contributing to identity development. Emotionally, this age group is developing a sense of competence. They are less egocentric and can see themselves with some level of objectivity. Parents and teachers influence the self-evaluations of this age group greatly, and children will internalize the criteria for self-evaluation established by these authority figures. They still have many fears, love ritual (e.g., incantation and repetition), and use it to help form group identity as well as to ward off some of their fears (Levine et al., 1983, pp. 108-132; Carnegie Corporation of New York, 1996).

Elementary school students tend to remember incidents and information at random, much like preschoolers do. They also have a difficult time selecting which facts or incidents are the most salient in a situation or plot. This is very important in terms of the types of computer programming that would be beneficial for this age group. With regard to the Internet, this age group would greatly benefit from information literacy training that could assist them in making good choices about what they are viewing on the Internet. Programming that would enrich their development would make the motives for actions and consequences for those actions evident, provide comprehensive and organized frameworks to help children perceive and understand the world, and highlight similarities and differences between people (Levine et al., 1983, pp. 108-132; Carnegie Corporation of New York, 1996).

The age group Singer suggested may be the most vulnerable to inappropriate online content is children ages 9-12. This age group begins to show great interest and curiosity about sex, and they develop crushes and hero worship. In general, this age group has not had much experience with sexuality, so online experiences are not tempered by real-life ones in any way. Peer groups begin to replace adults as the source of behavioral standards and recognition of achievement. They may feel frustrated and guilty if they cannot live up to standards they have set for themselves, and the opinions of their friends are important to their developing sense of self. Children of this age are beginning to become independent and tend to be a bit defiant of authority, especially when there appears to be a conflict between adult and peer conduct codes. In addition to having conflicts with adults, this age group often demonstrates their independence by exploring unknown places. They also may have passionate dependence on their best friend, suggesting that although they are differentiating from parents, they are not independent of relationships or not in need of support (Levine et al., 1983, pp. 108-132; Carnegie Corporation of New York, 1996).

Computer programming that Singer felt could nurture the development of 9-12-year-olds would take advantage of their ability to reason, play with abstract ideas, ambiguity, and speculation. Stimulating strategies of inquiry as well as providing an outlet for fantasy and imaginative play is also important as it becomes less socially acceptable for this age group to play make-believe publicly. Singer also stated that it is important for parents to try to maintain an open dialogue with children of this age, and that this is very important for helping them cope with the Internet. As this age group is developing an interest in exploration and independence, it may be more difficult to prevent them from going to an inappropriate web site—be it pornography or a site devoted to hate speech. Most beneficial would be relationships in which children felt they could come to their parents and talk about having viewed a disturbing web site—whether entirely accidentally or because they went there out of curiosity—and were not prepared for what they saw. A conversation after an experience such as this provides the parent the opportunity to comfort the child, discuss why the content is upsetting and objectionable, as well as to talk about how to avoid such material in the future.

Adolescents (ages 12-15) are changing rapidly and experience a wide range of fluctuating emotions. Physical changes can be disruptive to self-esteem and, combined with social pressure, may lead to problems of adjustment. Stress and conflict with parents, school, and friends are not uncommon as adolescents at once seek both independence by unconsciously wishing for control and limits set by authority. Curiosity about sexuality is very important to this age group, as is the desire to explore sexual relationships and to establish a sexual identity. Adolescents are vulnerable to media images in part because, as Jane Brown suggested, it offers a set of images and scripts against which to evaluate whether they are normal in terms of sexual expression, gender representation, or developing an attractive body (Levine et al., 1983, pp. 133-157; Steinberg, 1999, pp. 330-365).

Socially, adolescents have a strong need to feel accepted in peer groups and strive for a sense of belonging in both same-sex and mixed groups. Subcultures are developing in adolescent populations, and these subcultures are shaped by variations in meeting places, choices in literature and media sources, dating patterns, and Internet relationships and chat rooms. The values established by their families are retained during this period, but adolescents are questioning these ideas and considering what alternatives might mean for their lives. This exploration can make them vulnerable to a number of risk-taking behaviors, such as early sexual relationships and drinking. The combination of exploring alternatives to the values of their family and their need to belong can leave adolescents at risk for being drawn into radical sects (e.g., racist or violent groups). Girls tend to be more socially advanced than males not only because their bodies are more fully developed, but also because they are thinking carefully about what it means to be a woman, a mother, and family roles (Levine et al., 1983, pp. 133-157; Steinberg, 1999, pp. 242-273).

Beneficial computer programming would acknowledge the feelings, values, and dilemmas facing this group as well as the diverse and complex social realities of adolescent cultures. Singer suggested that programs show positive role-models of teens contributing to society in their own way, creating a wide spectrum of life possibilities so that adolescents can fantasize about what may exist for their futures. Ideally, these positive programs would be much more prevalent than negative alternatives that construct future realities that are not productive, that feed into adolescents concerns, or that offer solutions that represent risky behavior or have negative social consequences—for example, "solutions" to racial tension that center on themes of separatism or dominance.

Singer and others noted that telling adolescents where not to go online will often result in their going directly to that Internet site. Teaching young people to avoid material parents view as inappropriate is a foundation that must be laid at an earlier age. Open relationships in which an adolescent can come to discuss a problematic interaction in a chat room or a disturbing web site are more beneficial than strict filtering, according to Singer. She suggested that if a parent can recognize that their adolescent is curious about sexuality in a more adult way, and that this is a normal part of development, it might be possible to maintain an open dialogue in which the adolescent would be inclined to continue to turn to the parent for support and insight.

Moral Development

James Youniss of the Catholic University Life Cycle Institute provided an overview of moral development in young people, which also requires an early foundation for successful development. Children learn morality at a young age and can bring a strong moral framework to making decisions about where they go and how they interact with others online. Morality is developed primarily through interpersonal relationships that young people have with parents, caregivers, and peers (Dunn, 1987; Youniss, 1980).

Young children (ages 2-3) can differentiate clearly between right and wrong and recognize when they have behaved appropriately or badly. They become embarrassed and show pleasure, and they develop this awareness through the feedback they constantly receive from their relationship with their parents or primary caregiver. Young children also demonstrate the beginnings of moral behavior when they are with other children. This age group will automatically share a toy with another child, take turns, and talk to other children in a turn-taking fashion, all of which are early signs of moral development (Dunn, 1987; Youniss, 1980).

School-age children continue their moral development through their interpersonal relationships, although the precise way in which children learn about morality changes with their cognitive, social, and emotional development. While young children process feedback in a fairly straightforward and literal manner, school-age children develop a morality based on a complementary relationship with parents and a contrasting relationship with peers (Dunn, 1987; Youniss, 1980). For example, a six-year-old would explain that the way to be kind to one's parents is to obey them in some form, to be nice to them, or to do what they want. For a child of this age, primary caregivers appear omnipotent and omniscient, because they depend on caregivers for help with everything from when to get up, what clothes to wear to school, and what medicine will make you well. Children do not experience this dependence as oppressive because the caregiver is the one who helps them, and in turn the child wishes to please the caregiver by reciprocating some of this help by obeying (Damon, 1988; Youniss, 1980).

This age group also learns a sense of morality through a contrasting relationship with their peers. Youniss described this as a morality based on "when you are good to me, I'll be good to you." Children learn to share and reciprocate treatment based on the way peers treat them. This system is not entirely simple, however, because when children reach the ages of 8 to 10, they begin to realize that absolute adherence to this behavior code will end in a stalemate if power between the parties is equal. At that point, children begin to understand acts of omission as moral errors or events. For example, failing to help a friend who needs you (but perhaps has not done anything to help you at that moment) is now understood as a moral error. Group relationships among school-age children are characterized by a sense of democracy, fairness, and the application of rules that allows the group to redefine itself if they agree on a change (Damon, 1988; Youniss, 1980).

Youniss summarized these two forms of moral development in the following way. Children know how to get what they want from parents, and their morality is based on obtaining care and materials they need and want. The morality developed regarding their friends is one based on supporting the interests and needs of their friends so that they in turn will receive support in the future. Although it may appear somehow problematic that the foundations of moral development lie in promoting one's self-interests, Youniss stated that this is in fact normative, legitimate, and absolutely necessary in the process of developing a sense of morality.

Adolescents demonstrate significant changes in the way they build on their existing moral foundations. Youniss identified three significant shifts in the way in which adolescents learn about morality compared with younger children. First, the moral principles acquired from peers are injected into the parent-adolescent relationship. Adolescents now display and seek from parents trust, responsibility, and obligation. Adolescents fear parental judgments but tend to be more open with them about establishing rules and moral principle as long as parents are open in return. Adolescents will not accept a new moral principle without some explanation of why and the opportunity to participate in the establishment of that rule. The reciprocity that was established in peer relationships now applies to the caregiver-adolescent relationship. A more general morality is now formed, one based on shared authority and reciprocity in which peers and parents must always make their positions clear (Youniss and Smollar, 1985).

How should the Internet be considered in light of moral development? Youniss noted that one of the most important factors directing moral development is feedback from relationships with others (Youniss and Yates, 1999). Peers and parents can give positive and negative feedback, and both forms of feedback help young people develop a moral code. The Internet, however, will not necessarily provide negative feedback if a young person is engaged in an activity or conversation that is not moral. Thus it poses a problem for development.

That the Internet has no product that can be evaluated is another challenge for moral development. Feedback often stems from young people evaluating the outcome of an activity based on the product that emerges, such as consequences that all parties can observe and discuss (Youniss and Smollar, 1985). Because online activities can be done anonymously, in private, and without visible consequences, this typical avenue through which young people establish moral principles is unavailable. Youniss pointed out one factor that can help to mitigate this potentially negative aspect of the Internet: peers often share information about the Internet. They refer each other to web sites, they talk about what they have done and seen online. These discussions offer an opportunity for feedback and for peers to direct each other to positive online sites. Youniss pointed out that, although a prevalent belief in our culture is that "parents teach you what is right, and then peers come along and teach you all the deviance you know," this is not really true. Rather peers have very moral relationships with one another, they give each other good advice, they protect each other, and they try to make each other happy.

Youniss referred to Erik Erikson's work as a place to begin to understand how the Internet may figure into an adolescent's growing awareness of sexuality. Young adolescent explorations into sexuality are generally recognized as a process of self-exploration in which honest attempts at love really are not yet possible. The point is to discover one's sexual self and in what way sexuality fits into one's identity. Because of this, Youniss suggested that the exploration adolescents might do on the Internet might not be such a bad thing.

A balanced approach to adolescent online exploration was warranted, although Youniss preferred that the most lurid images (e.g., sexually violent images) were not readily accessible. Some of the extreme concern about sexually explicit material, he observed, was perhaps energy not well spent. Concerns are grounded in the notion that the Internet will change sexual behaviors. If this were the case, we should be seeing some change in the sexuality of youth, Youniss said. In fact, the past 5-6 years have shown a decline in sexual activity among youth and reduced rates of teen pregnancy, which is at its lowest rate in 40 years (National Center for Health Statistics, 1995, 1999). Positive trends have been observed in other fronts as well: school achievement has increased and marijuana use and violence have dropped. Youniss took all of these as positive indicators of the moral status of today's youth, suggesting that these are good signs that young people bring the type of moral character to the Internet that stands to create positive online communities and environments that can help to perpetuate—rather than negatively impact—morality.

Finally, Youniss commented on monitoring and how parents could balance keeping track of their children's online activities without violating their privacy. Recent literature on monitoring has been consistent suggesting that parents should not monitor through self-initiated actions (e.g., the online equivalent of reading a young person's diary); instead monitoring should come from the relationship between parent and child (Kerr and Statin, 2000). There is no easy or fast way to do this, but parents should strive for open communication with their children in which dialogue can occur. If a trusting relationship exists, young people will tell parents more and parents will be able to ask more probing questions and expect real answers. Monitoring must therefore occur in the context of the relationship, and through communication and discussion rather than policing, Youniss stated.

Social Norms Online

Patricia Greenfield, professor of psychology at the University of California, Los Angeles, discussed material young people could encounter on the Internet from a developmental perspective, considering both the material that users could passively browse as well as the material that users might create and construct. Increasing parents' awareness of a broader range of online material that she viewed as a concern as well as finding ways in which parents could influence the norms being established in children's online communities were the focus of her remarks. Greenfield was concerned about several areas, including sexually explicit content—which she defined much more broadly than pornographic web sites—as well as violence, aggression, hate speech, and advertising.

When most people think of pornography on the Internet, they imagine static web sites with sexually explicit images that appear on their computer screens in a similar manner to a magazine. Web sites of this type are available online and can range from images equivalent to those viewed in an R-rated movie to quite graphic, sexually violent images. In the case of the latter, a user almost always has to deliberately select a set of search words that would get them to these images, although many of those available are free and do not require age verification. However, searching for sexually explicit web sites is only one way to encounter—intentionally or unintentionally—sexually explicit material online. Images can be sent attached to emails, the addresses of which are often harvested when a user enters a chat room. In addition, individuals online can "instant message" one another, and those comments may be an innocuous introduction or something more lurid. Chat room talk can also be a source of sexually explicit material, although the nature of both chat and instant messaging is quite different from a sexually explicit web page: chat and instant messaging are interactive and textual, while web pages are static and image-oriented. What is perhaps particularly significant about chat rooms compared with web sites is that young people can participate and have greater control in the construction of sexuality that occurs in these cyberspaces. Although there are as yet no studies comparing the impact of sexually explicit web sites to participation in a chat room, other research on the media has suggested that interactive forms of media in which participants have greater control over the activity are more powerful than ones that are less participatory in nature (Calvert and Tan, 1994).

Greenfield voiced concern about the sexually explicit nature of the talk that she observed in chat rooms. Her first concern was that although chat rooms are very popular with young people, many parents have never been in a chat room and are entirely uninformed about the types of communication that occur in many of them. Greenfield offered examples of two different chat rooms she visited through major online portals. The first was an unmonitored chat room for teens, although there is no way to know the age of any user who enters this "space." In this chat room, Greenfield observed explicit sexual exchanges, joking about physical violence and assaults, degradation of other users, aggression, and a disturbing exchange involving racial stereotypes and prejudice. Although she participated in none of the exchanges, she was instant messaged six times with offers of technical assistance as well as sexual advances. In a monitored chat room for teens, the users engaged in similar exchanges, although their language was coded in order to get past censors. For example, one user asked for another user's "A/S/L," which translates as age, sex, and location.

A chat room for children under age 12 that Greenfield visited was more strictly monitored, and in fact when an exchange broke out between two users and the term "doo-doo face" was used to describe one of the users, the monitor interrupted, suspended the violator from the chat room for 15 minutes, reminding the user that this language could result in a permanent loss of chat room privileges, and asked that the user take that time to discuss online behavior with the user's parents. Although it would seem naïve to think that a scolded user would actually turn to his parents, being suspended from the chatroom is at least a material consequence.

Greenfield's point in this presentation was not to suggest that the exchange of crass words would irreparably damage a young person, but rather that the norms of acceptable behavior and communication established in these chat rooms were problematic. In general, the chat rooms she observed were outside societal norms of decency regarding the representation and discussion of sexuality, aggression, and intergroup relations. Sexuality in chat rooms and instant messaging were conducted in public rather than private, were linked to strangers, had little to do with relationships, were explicit, and were associated with the degradation of women.

For Greenfield, the context of chat rooms and instant messaging raised several developmental questions. How might the normative social standards in chat rooms affect young users? At what age can young people effectively handle sexual initiatives from strangers? What life skills, preparation, and savvy are needed to have to handle these situations? How does anonymity affect personal and social responsibility in online communities? As Greenfield pointed out, there are no scientific data on these questions, and one can only extrapolate from what is known about child development in general to speculate on the extent to which these issues pose an actual problem for development. What types of online activities constitute a normal and developmentally appropriate exploration into sexuality by adolescents? When can young users' experiments with different personas and forms of sexual expression be productive, and what, if any, interactions may lead to permissive attitudes toward sexual, aggressive, and prejudiced behavior, as well as the potential for early sexual priming before sexual maturity has been reached? Some basic content analyses are needed to document the types of cybercultures that exist and the way in which adult involvement can positively or negatively influence the social norms in these online communities.

USE PATTERNS OF THE INTERNET

Constructing effective strategies to protect kids on the Internet can benefit from a consideration of how young people are using the Internet. Janet Schofield, committee member and professor at the University of Pittsburgh, suggested that these questions about young people's Internet use could be characterized as supply and demand issues. With respect to supply, one can consider what type of content is widely available on the Internet. For instance, the extent to which pornography sites are available compared with sexual health and education is one example of analysis on the supply or availability side of the Internet. On the demand side, one can examine the types of activities young people engage in online, the extent to which they use the Internet, and for what purposes. Strategies to address supply or demand issues would certainly be very different. This section reviews material on young people's Internet and media use, for what purposes young people use the Internet, and how marketing may influence children's online activities.

Citing the Kaiser Family Foundation's report, *Kids & Media @ the New Millennium: A Comprehensive National Analysis of Children's Media Use* (1999), Donald Roberts, professor of communication at Stanford University, described what is known about the role of the media in kids' lives. The average child spends about 5.5 hours per day using media—be it television, radio, CDs, or the computer. Young people will use more than one form of media at once (e.g., listening to a CD while surfing the Internet), so children are doing a lot of parallel processing in their media use. Children ages 8-14 tend to spend more hours using media than teens ages 14-18. This is likely because of the busier and more diverse schedules of older teens (Roberts et al., 1999).

Perhaps surprisingly, time using the computer averaged only 31 minutes for children ages 8-18, with only a portion of that time devoted to online and Internet activities. Television, by far, was still the most commonly used form of media, and this age group had the television on an average of 3.25 hours per day. In this study 62 percent of children had a computer at home. Of families living in affluent communities in which the community income averaged above $40,000, 81 percent had computers compared to 49 percent of families in communities with an average income under $25,000. Schools seemed to mitigate some of these differences, often providing access for children who did not have a personal computer in their homes (Roberts et al., 1999).

Of the entire sample of young people surveyed, on average children spent only 21 minutes on the computer in recreation (32 minutes and 30 minutes for ages 8-13 and 14-18, respectively). Children used the computer primarily for games but did spend some time in chat rooms, sending email, and surfing web sites. Of the group of children who reported using the computer yesterday, games occupied the majority of their recreational time online. The 8-13-year-olds using a computer yesterday logged the longest average recreation times on the computer (over 1 hour), spending 32 minutes playing games, 14 minutes looking at web sites, 11 minutes in chat rooms, and 8 minutes sending emails (Roberts et al., 1999).

Most children's media use—including time on the computer and online—does not involve parental supervision. Many kids have radios, CD players, a television, and even a computer in their rooms, and Roberts viewed this as problematic. Although this may be relevant to disciplinary issues, it is certainly pertinent that parents are not monitoring their children's media activity, nor can they readily provide any feedback or support for children's online activities because they are using their computers in private.

Computers and Internet surfing do not make up the majority of children's media consumption by any yardstick, and in this respect television poses a much more significant influential factor in development, at least in terms of the sheer amount of time that young people spend with that form of media, Roberts noted. The amount of time they spend using computers and going online is likely to increase, however, as computer use continues to penetrate into homes and schools.

Sarah Keller, assistant professor of health communication at Emerson College, spoke of the dangers of economic predators on the Internet, such as marketers to children, and presented examples of market research tactics as possible models for educators. Data from a market survey by Grunwald Associates shows that more than 25 million children in the United States have access to the Internet, three times the number of children who were online in 1997, and representing 40 percent of American children 2 to 17 years old (<www.grunwald.com/survey/index.htm>). By 2005 it is estimated that almost 44 million children (ages 2-17) will be using the Internet. School access is expected to surpass home access by 2003 as classroom wiring initiatives are actuated. This study found that family decisions to purchase Internet access were centered on their children's educational needs, and, interestingly, children also cited education as their leading activity while online. Children tend to find out about interesting web sites from other children and other informal sources.

But, children's primary use of the Internet continues to be social. As in the Kaiser Family Foundation study, a survey from Pricewaterhouse Coopers E-Retail Intelligence System showed that email is a significant reason why teens go online, with half of the teens surveyed indicating that email was their primary reason for being online (<cyberatlas.internet.com/big_picture/demographics/article>). Although research on children's online behavior is scarce, a survey by Zandl Group of 8-12-year-olds with home Internet access showed that 80 percent of this age group play games, 72 percent use email, 58 percent chat or use message boards, 54 percent do school work, 42 percent download music, and 22 percent shop (Zollo, 1995). One other point of interest Keller noted is that a report by the Pew Internet and American Life Project found that about half of regular Internet users of any age (an estimated 52 million) use the Internet for information on health issues such as diseases, clinical trials, treatment, and nutrition, as well as for assistance in making health-related decisions (Richardson, 2000). As Brown and Keller both suggested, this may be of great significance with regard to young people and sexual health awareness.

SUMMARY

A great deal of information on children's media use was presented in the workshop. On average, young people are not spending significant portions of their time with a computer and spend even less time online (Roberts et al., 1999). This average is likely to increase as computers become even more widely available in schools and homes, and as different media forms (e.g., music, television, the Internet) become increasingly integrated and interrelated. In addition, as the number of devices that allow one to get online (e.g., cell phones and other hand-held transmitters) become more widely available, children will have new paths to the Internet. Not only will this increase use, but also these new tools may make screening material before it reaches a young person more difficult.

In the assessment of many of workshop participants, the only way to ensure that children are not harmed by inappropriate content was to arm the child rather than the computer. A young person who is taught strategies to stay in control of their online experiences, to be critical and skeptical about the underlying messages in advertising and romanticized and sexualized images, and to report users soliciting personal information brings that training to any device she or he uses and any venue in which she or he is getting online. Some speakers felt that filtering and monitoring under certain circumstances could be helpful, but for developmental reasons they were very careful to describe a specific context in which these strategies should be used. For example, Cantor suggested that allowing the young person to know the override code as a way to express trust in the young person's judgment and honesty was a good way to handle filtering. This provides an opportunity for the parent to teach the young person accountability for their actions by sharing the responsibility of the decision to keep the filter on while also providing a little leeway as a young person moved into adolescence and began to seek information about sexuality independently, information that might otherwise be screened out by a filter. Youniss emphasized that monitoring is best done by maintaining open communication and a trusting relationship between parent and child so that a parent could discuss online activities with the child and receive honest answers. Through this relationship the child might also be more comfortable coming to the parent after encountering material that concerned them. Youniss felt existing literature was clear that this dialogue was much more beneficial to children's development than for a parent to snoop through Internet log files to secretly see where a young person had gone online.

4

Nontechnical Strategies

> When our children are younger, we keep them in safe places. But we don't keep them in safe places until they are eighteen. We take them out into public. We teach them to recognize danger. We teach them the skills to deal with that danger, and, most importantly, we impart to them our values and our expectations for their behavior. As they grow, we step back and allow them the freedom to demonstrate to us that they have learned these skills, and can act in accordance with these values. We are always present for awhile, providing that necessary supervision, and when appropriate, discipline, and hopefully keeping the conversation alive, and continuing to discuss values and expectations.
>
> —Nancy Willard, workshop participant

Workshop participants heard presentations by both researchers and educators working to protect young people from sexually explicit and other inappropriate material on the Internet. The nontechnical strategies presented encompassed a variety of programs to educate parents and young people on Internet use. The majority of strategies focus on reducing young people's exposure to inappropriate material, while others center on providing them with skills to mitigate any possible effects they might experience from encountering sexually explicit or inappropriate material online. Some strategies also had implications for Internet safety by training young people to deal with interactions with other users.

A number of strategies and approaches to creating positive online experience for young people are presented in this chapter. These include social marketing strategies, media and information literacy, educational outreach to parents, monitoring and mentoring, acceptable use policies, responsible "netizenship," and professional development for educators. This chapter provides a conceptual description of each approach, defining it in a broad sense and then providing more specific examples of instances in which these concepts were put into practice. Many of the strategies discussed can be adapted to the specific contexts, needs, and constraints within which a community may be working, although some approaches may be more feasible for larger institutions than, for example, parents concerned about their children's home use or a revenue-strapped school. For each approach, a brief discussion is devoted to identifying the contexts (e.g., home, school, libraries) or type of institution that might effectively put a strategy into place. It is important to note that many of the conceptual approaches can be adapted to particular circumstances with a little ingenuity. The particular material targeted (e.g., Internet safety, reducing exposure to sexually explicit material, recognizing and resisting direct marketing) is also explored. Again, many strategies may be used to address a number of issues online, and readers are encouraged to evaluate these strategies with their own needs and contexts in mind. Table 4-1 displays the range of strategies, the contexts in which these approaches have been effective, the feasibility of the strategy and who would need to support it, and material the strategies target.

SOCIAL MARKETING STRATEGIES

Sarah Keller used the term "social marketing" to describe several approaches that center on reducing young people's exposure to inappropriate material by increasing the amount and accessibility of positive, educational material on the Internet. An online landscape filled with productive, stimulating, and developmentally beneficial material was seen as an important objective by many workshop participants, many of whom decried the dearth of educational material online and a need for greater funding for developing such online curricula. This landscape would include more web sites devoted to sexual health and education, so that curious adolescents could get reliable information on sexuality rather than, or at least before, finding sexually explicit material lacking information or depicting unprotected sex or other unsafe sexual practices. Others suggested that creating web sites, portals, or even a zone with a domain name ending in ".kids" and filling it with developmentally appropriate, educational, and enjoyable material on a broad range of appealing topics. These portals or a ".kids" domain could make child-friendly material more readily accessible.

TABLE 4-1 Chart of Nontechnical Strategies

Strategy	Context (Home, School, Library)	Feasibility/Collaboration Required	Type of Inappropriate Content Targeted
Social Marketing Strategies			
Variations			
• ".kids" domain	Always available on the Internet so works in all contexts. However, child must choose to go to this content while online.	Potentially costly, requires collaboration of industry, foundations, government, etc., to fund development.	Because links are preselected, it can prevent exposure from any inappropriate material. Offers positive content and could increase amount of material on sexual health, but does not prevent young people from accessing other material.
• Portal to the Web (homepage with links)	Always available, but child must choose to use the portal. This is more likely to occur in a supervised situation (e.g., classroom in which students are directed to work from specific home page).	Schools, libraries, and other community institutions can accomplish if individuals with some technical expertise are available.	Same as above.
Media and Information Literacy			
• Curricula	Strengthens resistance to inappropriate Internet content and therefore functions in any context in which the child is online.	Most applicable for schools and library programs. Costs associated with curriculum development and instructor labor.	Curricula can be designed to address any specific type of content (sexually explicit, violent, hate speech, misleading content, etc.).

Educational Outreach

Variations

• Public awareness (campaign via television)	NA	Campaigns could focus on any content issue, but likely to be most effective in raising parents awareness about Internet safety.
	Costly, funding needed from industry, foundations, and/or government.	
• Online training	NA	Same as above.
	Nonprofit organizations, industry, and government agencies can all design sites.	
• Hands-on training	NA	Same as above.
	Community groups, schools, and libraries are positioned to offer training.	

Monitoring and Mentoring

Variations

• Use of space to facilitate supervision	Useful in classrooms, libraries, homes, community centers—any context in which supervision is possible.	Does not guard against specific content. Success depends on the attentiveness of supervisors.
	No cost, teachers, librarians, and parents can do this.	
• Sign-up sheets to promote accountability	Useful in situations for multiple users (schools and libraries).	Does not guard against specific content. Potential deterrent to kids looking for inappropriate content.
	No cost, success depends on students' reaction to lack of anonymity.	
• Cyber navigator mentoring	Schools, libraries, and community groups can institute programs.	Can protect against any type of content, but success depends on the attentiveness of supervisors.
	Low cost, programs can use volunteers, drawing in particular on older high schoolers and college students.	

continues

TABLE 4-1 Continued

Strategy	Context (Home, School, Library)	Feasibility/Collaboration Required	Type of Inappropriate Content Targeted
Acceptable Use Policies			
Variations			
• School policy	Behavior expectations can only be enforced in school, so students may or may not feel compelled to follow these expectations beyond school use.	Fairly simple, individual teachers can establish class expectations. More collaboration and planning is needed for school-wide or district-wide policy, though it is still low cost.	Policy can be designed to establish behavior expectations for many different types of content.
• Home use agreement between parent and child	Could protect children in any context if policy is conveyed in a manner that tells the child the behavior expected at all times.	No cost, parent must be informed to address this issue and establish behavior expectations.	Same as above.
Responsible Netizenship			
	Once taught, it could protect children in any context if they are committed to these safety standards.	No or low cost, can be incorporated into acceptable use policies in schools and by parents.	Internet safety, interactive content and contact with other users.

Professional Development

Variations:

• Changes to teacher training in universities	NA	Costly, restructuring teacher training to include greater facility with technology is a needed but long range plan and will require funding by universities and government.	Curricula can be designed to train teachers to address many types of content. Information and media literacy would be a useful component.
• Continuing education	NA	Moderate cost, in service days could provide Internet safety and content as topics. Universities and other organizations could also design continuing education classes.	Same as above.

47

Social marketing strategies such as these would help to keep young people away from pornography and other inappropriate material by providing a venue that meets their needs and interests. By increasing the number of sites or creating a domain name dedicated to children, easily searchable, and convenient (e.g., homework help to guide students to relevant information), young people might choose to go to these sites voluntarily, which in turn would keep them away from objectionable material. Parents might also have an easier time directing their children's Internet use by directing their children to surf only the ".kids" domain.

Sarah Keller identified three benefits in adopting a social marketing approach. First, by providing better educational and more healthful content, the burden of regulating and screening content is reduced. Schools could use portals to these educational sites, which might reduce the costs of filtering and screening if they could provide an online platform that went directly to these useful cyberspaces.

Second, although educating parents and encouraging them to be responsible and involved in their children's online activities is an important and viable strategy, it is difficult to accomplish. Social marketing alleviates the difficulty to some extent by reaching young people directly. These web sites could easily include information on online safety as well as other educational content.

Third, evaluating educational web sites and portals is more feasible than trying to evaluate online content as a whole. As an example, Keller described the evaluation process of the teen web site, <iwannaknow.org>, a project she and Jane Brown are currently involved in. This process began with a content analysis that compares the information available on the site to the recommendations established by the Sexuality Information and Education Council of the U.S. (SIECUS), a recognized authority on sex education (Keller et al., 2000). The analysis was used to create an online survey to measure the site's impact on teen knowledge, attitudes, and intended behaviors. Furthermore, the site was evaluated using the American Library Association's recommendations on navigability, accuracy, authority, currency, and objectivity (Kapoun, 2000). Keller said this example demonstrates that educational content can be evaluated in a manner that is thorough, rigorous, and feasible and can grapple with the extent to which a site is developmentally appropriate, relevant to young people's needs and interests, and user-friendly.

Striving for better, thoroughly evaluated educational online content will take time. The creation of a ".kids" domain, for example, would take time and could be costly. Smaller-scale attempts to create a socially appropriate and educationally beneficial Internet landscape for children also have potential because they can be accomplished more quickly and on a local basis, though they will inevitably have significantly less material than a ".kids" domain could.

Mary Dempsey, commissioner of the Chicago Public Library, described the Chicago Public Library's effort to create a kids-safe portal to the web. The library's home page for kids and teens is designed to be a safe portal to that links to educational material online. The page, Chicago Public Library Sign of the Owl (<www.chipublib.org/008subject/003cya/sign/sign.html>), has an attractive graphic with a flashing button for an Internet safety quiz as well as a menu that includes the Teen Edition, Homework Help, Good Reads and Great Books, as well as resources for parents, teachers, and youth librarians. The Safety Quiz is an interactive quiz that poses one question at a time that can be answered with a yes or no button that calls up the correct response as well as feedback about the question. For example, the second question in the quiz is "If I see stuff on the Internet that makes me uncomfortable should I keep it a secret?" Depending on your answer you either get a bouncing star graphic (if you are correct) or a "Danger" sign if you answer incorrectly. Both answers are accompanied by the following text: "If you are at home, tell your parents right away if you come across any information that makes you feel uncomfortable. If you are at the public library, tell a librarian and then leave that page right away." This short quiz is fun (even for adults) and provides very useful information about Internet safety to children, Dempsey said. In addition, the links provided on the Sign of the Owl home page are helpful and entertaining, and the Homework Help section is useful to students.

The Sign of the Owl, with a reasonably extensive number of links, is an example of a positive "kids area," or what some have likened to the Public Broadcasting Service's (PBS) children's television programming, but created for an online venue. Creating a home page for a school or library that acts as a portal to the web is not difficult. In the simplest form, a teacher would preselect material relevant to a class by bookmarking a series of sites in a navigator or simply providing a list of sites that students should use for a unit or project. Creating an area dedicated to young people and filled with educational material could be a very ambitious project, such as creating an expansive ".kids" domain filled with enough interesting material that young people can get immersed in for hours, or it could be a relatively low-tech effort to satisfy busy students with bookmarked sites, thus providing readily available links to prescreened material. Such approaches can be used now to create home pages with preselected lists of relevant sites, and it can also stimulate future development of positive content. This approach would avoid some of the difficulties associated with filtering and free speech issues.

Workshop participants suggested several models for funding larger projects, such as creating a ".kids" domain. One suggestion was joint ventures between foundations and the government to set up a media lab that would generate this material. A second suggestion was to call for the industry to earmark a certain amount of money to creating and managing a PBS-like site. Laurie Lipper, director of The Children's Partnership, compared this suggestion to the process that cable networks went through to create and support CSPAN. Although these projects are never entirely without self-interest on the part of the industry, she stated, like CSPAN, it is possible to create a useful and valuable product through this type of industry commitment.

Social marketing has the potential to protect young people from many types of inappropriate material because it selects and produces carefully considered educational and entertaining material for them. Internet safety can also be incorporated into safe portals so that young people will be exposed to this information when they go online. Social marketing has the additional benefit of avoiding issues pertaining to free speech because it centers on producing and making available material, rather than censoring or restricting certain types of content. The limitations of this approach are the potential costs of creating a large-scale ".kids" domain, and, in the case of creating individual portals to the web, the need for individuals with technical proficiency to generate homepages. Young people also may not be willing to work within the ".kids" domain even if they like the content contained in it. Because of this, social marketing would need to be paired with other approaches that involve parents or other authority figures setting rules and limits on young people's Internet use. Examples of these approaches appear later in the chapter in the sections on mentoring and monitoring and creating acceptable use policies.

MEDIA AND INFORMATION LITERACY

As noted earlier, every panel and nearly every panelist at the workshop stated that media and information literacy offer a particularly important and powerful set of strategies to protect young people from a wide range of inappropriate material online. Media literacy represents a set of skills required to critically analyze images and information represented in the media in order to evaluate the extent to which they are relevant and credible. For example, concept-oriented communication stresses the development of consumer competence and may be associated positively with adolescents' skepticism toward advertising and other harmful media content. In one study, mothers whose family communication patterns were based on concept orientation tended to mediate the media's influence on children by discussing and viewing ads with children (Carlson et al., 1992). A related study by Alemi et al. (1989) developed a computer program to allow teenage girls to practice making choices to prevent pregnancy. The feedback and information provided by the game to the teens allowed the girls to think critically about the contexts presented and practice decision making.

Information literacy describes the how-to skills of finding relevant and useful information on the Internet. For example, performing an effective search requires the selection of the right set of keywords, familiarity with Boolean logic, choosing the right search engine for the topic, and knowing how to navigate through a browser so that it is easy to enter and exit web sites, databases, and other online resource tools. Information literacy provides a set of strategies that could help to prevent young people from viewing inappropriate material in the first place (e.g., if a search returned a web site that the young person had learned to recognize was likely to contain sexually explicit material rather than information on reproduction, the user could simply choose not to click the questionable site).

The skills required to evaluate Internet content are a bit more challenging than those a young person would need to watch television critically. One of the primary differences is that many web sites provide what appears to be informational content but is in fact advocacy that may or may not be founded on research. Young people have a very difficult time telling the difference between compelling rhetoric and a compelling argument based on knowledge, and these are extremely important skills for today's children to acquire. Media literacy offers a set of cognitive skills that could protect against misleading information or a disturbing image by teaching young people how to recognize underlying messages, criticize them, and develop productive counternarratives (Mangleburg and Bristol, 1998). Finally, participants observed that media literacy could equip young people to deal with a wide variety of dangerous or inappropriate material online. Many viewed this as very important because they felt the attention to sexually explicit web sites comes at the cost of neglecting material that could be equally or more dangerous to young people because it encouraged them to make bad decisions about their behavior.

Joanne Cantor and Sarah Keller offered two studies of how media literacy can help counteract negative effects that young people may incur from their media consumption. Cantor conducted a study with elementary schoolchildren to determine if she could mitigate the aggression-promoting effect that research has shown often occurs with watching television violence. Investigators showed their young participants a violent cartoon but beforehand asked them to think about the feelings of the victim of violence throughout the episode. Viewers who received these instructions did not experience an increase in their acceptance of violent solutions to problems, nor did they find the cartoon to be as funny as those not instructed. This media literacy intervention reduced desensitization compared with the control group in the study (Nathanson and Cantor, 2000).

Keller conducted an online media intervention program with girls in their early teens designed to get them to think critically about the messages the media was providing about what women should think about romance, love, and sexuality (Keller, 2000). She asked the participants in the study to think critically about images they observed in the media and to identify how they thought the media was shaping their thoughts and attitudes about love, romance, and sexuality. The girls responded by criticizing the media because they felt the media encouraged them to focus too much on romance and trying to attract men. Their critical comments were used to help generate a web site with alternative images and messages that the teens thought reflected their own attitudes and experience with romance. The web site was pretested with 46 middle- and low-income girls of mixed ethnicities in New York City. Results indicate that recognizing the messages inherent in the media and being able to criticize those messages are important steps in being able to resist those messages, she said.

While such findings suggest that media literacy can help mitigate the impact of the media on young people's attitudes, the question remains of how to use media literacy in schools. Kathy Boguzewski, an instructional technology consultant with the Wisconsin Department of Public Instruction, described how she used media literacy to teach students how to evaluate information on the Internet in two different contexts. The first took place earlier in her career as a library specialist. The only connection to the Internet was in the library, thus Boguzewski had a great deal of control over the way in which the Internet was being used, and it was relatively easy to ensure that students were not only avoiding inappropriate material, but were obtaining useful and effective online resources. Students used the Internet almost exclusively for research purposes, and their time was limited because access was available only in the library. Boguzewski would begin by talking to students about their topics and would then teach them search strategies to help them find relevant information online. Once they had found several web sites, Boguzewski would teach the students how to evaluate the information they found to determine if it came from a reliable source and if the information was accurate and reasonable. Some of the questions used to guide their evaluation included:

1. Who wrote the information and what is the author's point of view?
2. Is the author identified and can you email the author?
3. Have you ever heard of the author/organization/company, and do you know what they stand for?
4. Is the information current and is a date given on the page?
5. Why is the information online—to inform or educate, to sell something, to entertain, or to push a particular point of view?
6. Are there links to other web pages and do they reveal any biases of the author?
7. Have any obvious links been omitted and are those provided relevant and reliable?
8. Who is the intended audience of the web site and how does its material compare with other web sites about the same topic?
9. Can you find something similar in the library that supports the information on the web page?

Boguzewski offered an example of how these questions can help teach young people how to be skeptical about information presented online and how to structure an analysis of it. Recalling a high school student who needed to write a persuasive paper and had chosen the legalization of marijuana as his topic, Boguzewski described the process she guided him through in order to differentiate valid information online from advocacy or misinformation. The student wanted to argue that marijuana should be legal and was generally an advantageous, if misunderstood, drug. Boguzewski did not judge him, but rather helped him to find web sites addressing this issue. After being disappointed by information on the American Medical Association (AMA) web site, which does not support legalization of this drug for a variety of medical and public health concerns, the student found a web site advocating for legalization. This particular teen was most pleased with his discovery until Boguzewski began to walk him through an analysis of the content offered on both sites. The teen recognized the AMA as an authority on scientific and medical knowledge and acknowledged that this information was pertinent to making evaluations of the benefits or negative consequences of using cannabis. In contrast, the web site advocating for legalization was published by a group that the student did not recognize and could not determine on what medical information the web site was basing its pro-cannabis position. Boguzewski suggested that the student email the contact person on the web site to ask why their position was in direct opposition to the AMA's regarding what the group identified as the benefits of cannabis. Unfortunately for the young pro-cannabis activist, the group did not reply to his email, so he had no other information through which to evaluate the credibility of the web site. Furthermore, the student agreed with Boguzewski that the questionable web site did not provide enough relevant or scientifically credible information to be preferred over that provided by the AMA, and therefore he could not use the web site as a basis for his argument.

In this example, Boguzewski taught both information literacy skills (e.g., using search engines effectively and selecting the most pertinent hits returned in the search) as well as media literacy (e.g., evaluating the extent to which information is relevant and credible). This was very effective in a one-on-one situation and allowed the opportunity for the adolescent to explore his views on a controversial topic in a controlled manner, forcing him to confront his assumptions while also learning the difference between web sites presenting research findings and compelling rhetoric. The limitation of this strategy is that it is time- and labor-consuming and in a one-on-one format would not be effective in a setting in which young people had extensive access to the Internet. However, one can imagine a computer classroom setting in which this experience could be translated into a lesson plan that walks a group of students through a web search and then as a group evaluates web sites that assume different positions on a particular topic.

As the availability of Internet access grew, one-on-one student lessons were not enough. Boguzewski began to train teachers in her school the strategies she had developed for evaluating information online so that they could use this process in their classrooms. The school institutionalized this process by including information literacy as an objective for student research papers—information drawn from online sources had to be thoroughly evaluated by the student, and this had to be demonstrated satisfactorily to the teacher. As access to the Internet has continued to grow in Wisconsin schools, a statewide policy about the use of technology was developed. This included an acceptable use policy to which all students must adhere as well as a series of developmental, educational objectives for the technology skills that must be mastered by a student by specific grades. For example, by 4th grade, students must be able to use web sites preselected and bookmarked by the teacher; by 8th grade, they must know effective search strategies; and by the end of 12th grade, they must be able to evaluate Internet content for validity and reliability as well as to assess the search engines for effectiveness and the way in which they returned information. Boguzewski stated that this plan is of great benefit to students because it teaches them a life skill through information and media literacy, which they will need in college and other settings that do not have filters or adults to provide critical evaluations.

As strategies to protect young people from inappropriate material, media and information literacy offer a number of benefits: they teach young people critical thinking, knowledge evaluation, and skillful use of the Internet (e.g., effective searching), which may make them resistant to a wide variety of media influences (e.g., messages that could encourage unsafe sexual practices or other risky behaviors as well as commercialism and direct marketing). Once taught, these critical thinking skills stay with the child and can be used in any other setting involving the Internet. In other words, children are always armed against inappropriate material, even if the particular computer terminal they are using is unfiltered or is in a situation without adult supervision. The limitations of media and information literacy are that it can be time- and labor-intensive, especially if one considers creating a school-based curriculum, and it does depend on young people's cognitive skills. For example, while a younger child could be taught effective search strategies, depending on his or her developmental maturity, advanced critical thinking skills may or may not be within his or her reach. An adolescent, however, can be more easily taught critical and evaluative skills, as his or her cognitive skills are likely to be much more advanced.

EDUCATIONAL OUTREACH TO PARENTS

The workshop discussed the avenues for educational outreach to parents to raise awareness of the importance of being involved with their children's online activities and creating more opportunities for parents to increase their technological skills. The first objective of educational outreach is to raise parents' awareness about safety issues on the Internet that they need to discuss with their children. Many participants observed that the most effective way to accomplish this would be through a national public awareness campaign. Anne Thompson reminded the audience of the awareness campaign in the late 1980s, "It's eleven o'clock. Do you know where your kids are?" She suggested that a similar television campaign might be effective, offering the following slogan, "It's eleven o'clock. Do you know where your kids are online?"

This type of campaign would certainly reach a wide audience especially if television were the platform to reach people. It could pique parent interest, convey a few points of information, and refer parents to additional information. A drawback to this approach is that it would be an expensive endeavor and is likely to need support from a number of collaborating institutions. A less expensive means to accomplish this would be to create educational web sites, as The Children's Partnership has done (outlined below). However, only parents who are already online and perhaps seeking information would be reached.

In addition to raising parent awareness of this issue, workshop participants commented that there is also a great need for more in-depth training. Improving parents' efficacy with technology and "cyber parenting" are two extremely important areas of training and represent more difficult tasks, requiring a more hands-on intervention than a public awareness campaign. There are existing models, largely from nonprofit organizations, that have worked to both identify the specific concerns and needs of parents as well as to develop programs that would provide training to increase their efficacy with the Internet. Both Laurie Lipper, co-director of The Children's Partnership, and Eileen Faucette, founder and coodinator of PTA Live Online, discussed outreach programs that their organizations have developed to assist parents in guiding their children's online activities, as well as the concerns parents have about the Internet and technology in general.

Outreach and Training Through the Internet

Children and technology became an important issue for The Children's Partnership almost immediately after opening in 1994. The mission of this organization is to identify emerging national issues that will impact large numbers of American children, particularly those who are already at risk. According to Lipper, outreach to parents about this issue is extremely important because they are often the only adult available to be responsible for their children's online activities and media habits. They are also important players in leveraging schools and other institutions that serve kids both at the local and national levels.

That parents feel inadequate or incapable of providing guidance or setting boundaries about their children's online activities was identified by both Lipper and Faucette as a big impediment to children's safety on the Internet. From her research with parents, Lipper consistently heard concerns from them that their children know so much more about computers than they do, and that they did not feel like they could provide any relevant guidance for them. Yet researchers in this workshop noted that parents' involvement in their children's media activities are beneficial for their development.

In response to parents' desire for information to teach their children online safety, The Children's Partnership developed *The Parent's Guide to the Information Superhighway*, first published in 1996. The report focuses on how parents need to think about and approach technology, as well as how they can address Internet issues with their children. It is not a how-to manual on filters or web support, but rather offers guidelines and recommendations on age-appropriate strategies for setting limits and encouraging productive online activities for children. A summary of these guidelines is presented in Box 4-1. The guide includes practical tools available to help foster parent-child discussion about online safety and responsible online behavior. For example, the report contains a sample contract for the parent and child to sign that lists some dangerous activities the child agrees never to do (e.g., never give out one's full name, address, or telephone number or agree to a face-to-face meeting with another user). This is a useful pedagogical tool, especially for parenting younger children, because it provides a concrete set of rules and boundaries for safe and acceptable behavior that parents and children can review and commit themselves to. The guide also discusses how the Internet can be used to emphasize a family's own values through a relational and educational process between parent and child.

The Children's Partnership web site posts the guide along with several other resources for parents, including a step-by-step look at what parents can do to work with their children. The guide is also available as a Microsoft powerpoint presentation guide that can be downloaded and used in training. At the time of the workshop, the organization was in the process of posting the results of a national survey on best practices for parent involvement in technology programs and locally available parent training. The Children's Partnership also helped initiate several community technology centers in low-income areas with programs to teach parents and children how

BOX 4-1
Age-Based Tips for Guiding Children's Home Internet Use

The Children's Partnership's *The Parents' Guide to the Information Superhighway* contains a wealth of practical suggestions and information for parents to consider as they make choices that affect their children's Internet use and online activities. The guide notes that while there is little research on the impact of technology on children, it is possible to offer some practical suggestions based on the advice of child development experts for setting age-appropriate guidelines for children's computer use. The following represents an abbreviated list of some of the suggestions contained in the guide. A complete copy of the guide is available at <www.childrens partnership.org>.

Ages 2-3: Computers need not play much of a role in the youngest child's life. However, it doesn't hurt for very young children to see family members using computers and enjoying themselves online. Tips: (1) Put your child in your lap as you "play" on the computer. (2) Look for books and children's video programs like Sesame Street that include images of children and family members using a computer.

Ages 4-7: While serious computer use isn't a priority for these youngsters, children at this age can begin to make greater use of computer games and educational products. Tips: (1) Spend as much time as you can with your child while he or she uses the computer. (2) Show lots of tangible results and achievements. For example, print work your child has done on the computer. (3) Share an email address with your child, so you can oversee his or her mail and discuss correspondence.

Ages 8-11: This age is when children can begin to directly experience and appreciate more fully the potential of online experiences. For instance, children can begin to use online encyclopedias, download pictures for school reports, or have email pen pals. Tips: (1) Set very clear rules for online use and clear consequences if they are broken. (2) Teach children to let you know if they encounter anything scary or unusual online. (3) Discuss some of the unique aspects of behavior in cyberspace—like anonymity and what it means for your child and for others.

Age 12-14: At this age, young people can use the more sophisticated research resources of the information superhighway, accessing everything from the Library of Congress's collection to magazines and newspapers to archives from around the world. Tips: (1) Since children this age are more likely to explore on their own, set up clear parental rules, limits, and periodic check-ins. (2) Set clear rules about which chat rooms are acceptable for your teenager, and how much time can be spent there. (3) Be sure your children understand the actions that can be taken if people harass them online or do anything inappropriate. (4) Pay particular attention to games that your teenager might download or copy as some of these games are extremely violent.

Ages 15-18: The Internet provides a rich resource for older teens, including information about job opportunities, internships, and colleges; applications to create multimedia reports; and specialized help with foreign languages and other school subjects. Tips: (1) Ask your teenager for help researching topics of interest to the family (follow-up on a family discussion, planning a family vacation, etc.). (2) Talk to your teenager about new things online and encourage discussion of new experiences. (3) Make sure your teenager knows the legal implications of online behavior. (4) Watch time limits to make sure your teenager is still pursuing a well-rounded set of activities. (5) If your teenager is especially interested in computers, encourage him or her to help younger children with their online explorations (e.g., at the local Boys or Girls Club).

to use the Internet and how to be safe online. The home page of The Children's Partnership links to many of these centers as a additional resource.

The Children's Partnership also conducted a series of focus groups with parents to find out what assistance they want with regard to the Internet. The information from these focus groups offers insight into programs that could prove effective in reaching a broader range of parents. In every focus group parents wanted to see a children-only zone with entertaining and educational material that was commercial free. Parents also requested information on important online issues that could accompany their monthly Internet bill or be emailed by their provider. Low-income parents expressed a great interest in more help from schools and teachers in offering education for both children and their parents. Parents also said they would like to see the industry set aside money to fund research on issues pertaining to children and the media.

Hands-On Training

Eileen Faucette's Live Online program started in response to local interest within the Fort Gordon, Georgia, community to provide a hands-on orientation to the Internet for parents. Live Online is a series of classes that include topics such as keeping kids safe and productive on the Internet, street smarts for the info highway, email ins and outs, search skills, and online literacy. The objectives of these classes are not to make parents more adept with the computer than their children, but rather to provide parents with enough exposure to the Internet that they feel confident talking with their children about their Internet activities and can set boundaries for activities. Creating effective cyberparents is the goal of the Live Online program, and Faucette tailors the classes to the interests and particular needs of the communities to which she travels. Sometimes Live Online is a series of topical classes, while at other times, Faucette will provide a single demonstration and presentation to raise awareness. Live Online is offered at a number of different locations depending on the needs of the community. A Barnes & Noble bookstore was the location of choice for the Fort Gordon community, while others have taken place at schools, community centers, and even at local businesses.

While Live Online serves to educate parents willing to attend a demonstration or class, Faucette had another strategy for conducting outreach with parents who were technophobes or who were unaware of the need to be involved in their children's Internet activities. Faucette's Sneak A-Tech programming involved taking computers to venues that had little to do with technology. For example, Faucette arranged to have computers and an Internet connection at a ladies gardening class and showed the group how to find information about planting, particular flower varieties, and seed availability. Faucette then used the opportunity to bring up issues related to young people, the Internet, and parenting to which the women were considerably more receptive after they had discovered that the Internet was not difficult to deal with and was even relevant to their own interests. She was able to sneak in a technology lesson in a nonthreatening way that the members of the gardening class enjoyed and were receptive to. With many adults, this is a very important first step toward becoming effective cyberparents.

Information, training, and hands-on activities such as those offered by The Children's Partnership and PTA Live Online can fill a knowledge gap and thereby assist parents in taking a more active role in their children's online activities. They may do a particularly good job of helping to address Internet safety with parents, although certainly programs could be tailored to facilitate approaches for parents to counteract other types of inappropriate material. The limitations of these projects reflect parents' willingness and ability to participate in such programs as well as their ability to make parents aware of the availability of such resources. Funding, of course, is always a challenge to such efforts.

MONITORING OR MENTORING

Monitoring and mentoring represent two sets of strategies that can be used in virtually every context. Schools, libraries, and parents can develop ways to monitor young people's online activities and can provide mentoring opportunities—parents can join their children in Internet surfing, and teachers or aides can work one-on-one with students.

Researchers in youth development in attendance at the workshop gave mixed reviews of monitoring as a strategy, stating clearly that its effectiveness depends largely on the particular way in which adults choose to monitor. They stressed the importance of parents being involved and knowing what their kids are doing online. However, they noted that the covert way of monitoring—looking secretly at a file log to determine the child's online visits—can violate trust. Instead, researchers suggested that using monitoring as a way to interact and even mentor young people would be a beneficial approach.

Mary Dempsey had several suggestions as to how parents, teachers, and librarians can keep an eye on children's online activities without being intrusive. One option Dempsey mentioned is Cyber Navigators, a program in the Chicago Public Libraries that offers a double benefit by providing personalized monitoring as well as mentors for young people. Cyber Navigators are college students who volunteer to help users with computer technology in the library. After receiving a week of training, they then help young users with the Internet by steering them to beneficial and educational sites, such as the National Science Foundation's web site or Ask Dr. Universe. Young people learn about the Internet and have the opportunity to interact with college students who can be role models. Their monitoring keeps children away from inappropriate or nonenriching material while providing a mini-lesson on Internet use and navigation.

Practical tools that help facilitate this type of monitoring include the physical setup and location of the computer. In the Chicago Public Libraries, Internet terminals in the children's area are arranged in a way that allows a librarian to see all of the monitors. In contrast, Internet terminals for adults in the rest of the library have privacy screens so that a young person cannot see an adult's activities, but librarians and Cyber Navigators can see what young people are doing online.

Parents can adapt this strategy at home by keeping the computer in a central location, such as the kitchen or family room, rather than in the privacy of the child's room. A classroom can be set up in a similar manner to the children's section of the library, in that computers can be situated to face the interior of the room so that the monitors are visible. In addition, sign-up sheets can be used to keep track of who is using the computer. In Chicago's libraries this is a necessity due to limited resources (i.e., the number of children wanting to get online exceeds the available computers so the sign-up sheet serves to regulate use). Dempsey observed that the sign-up sheet gives young users a sense of responsibility about how they spend their time online, because they cannot feel that they are anonymous users.

Such monitoring strategies as orienting a computer screen so that it is easily viewed by an adult in the room are easy to employ and come at no cost to teachers or parents. Volunteer programs, such as Dempsey's Cyber Navigators, also are virtually cost-free for institutions such as libraries if they have a volunteer pool from which to draw. In addition, Cyber Navigators or approaches like this program provide opportunities for mentoring relationships. Supervision does require the presence of an adult, but this can be turned into a time for adults and young people to interact and talk about numerous types of inappropriate material and safety issues.

ACCEPTABLE USE POLICIES

An approach to the Internet that can be used in any context in which young people are online is teaching them to be responsible for making good choices about the paths they choose in cyberspace by teaching them acceptable use and then trusting them to make responsible choices. Conveying expectations and boundaries for use to children is a task that any adult can do.

A more formalized version of this process is captured in acceptable use policies, a set of guidelines and expectations about how young people will conduct themselves online that are increasingly common in schools. These policies—an example of which is presented in Box 4-2—vary from school district to school district based on the particular concerns of teachers and parents, but in general they instruct young people that surfing sexually explicit web sites is not appropriate. Increasingly, acceptable use policies also address the material students post and publish online as well. Nancy Willard, director of Responsible Netizen Research at the Center for Advanced Technology in Education, University of Oregon, noted that it is not uncommon for young people themselves to create and disseminate sexually

BOX 4-2
Acceptable Use Policy of Eau Claire Area School District

The Eau Claire Area School District offers a good example of policies that establish a set of expectations about the manner in which students and staff will use school networks and technologies. This acceptable use policy sets rules about a number of topics, including guidelines to facilitate safety online, respecting copyrighted material—relevant to preventing students from using the Internet's resources to plagiarize material—as well as forbidding users from using the Internet for activities that are not in support of the educational objectives of the school district. What follows is a summary of the Eau Claire Area School District's acceptable use policy, the full text of which can be found at <www.ecasd.k12.wi.us/departments/technology/network/inetpol.html>.

Use of the Internet and Other Computer Networks

The Internet is an electronic network connecting thousands of computer networks and millions of individual subscribers all over the world. Access to the Internet will allow students to explore the rich resources of thousands of university libraries, governmental databases, and other online sources while exchanging electronic mail with Internet users throughout the world. Instructional and library materials are routinely evaluated by school district personnel prior to purchase in order to ascertain that such materials are consistent with district goals and guidelines and that they support and enrich the curriculum. However, use of the Internet, because it may lead to any publicly available fileserver in the world, may open classrooms to electronic information resources that have not been screened by educators for use by students. Some items accessible via the Internet may contain material that is inaccurate, defamatory or offensive. Access to the Internet and other computer networks requires that school officials develop guidelines for use. Such guidelines should address the teacher's responsibility for training and guidance, the student's responsibility for appropriate use, and the principal's responsibility for supervising the use.

Appropriate Use Guidelines

The following guidelines define "appropriate use" of the Internet.

1. All use of school resources to access the Internet must be in support of and consistent with the educational objectives of the Eau Claire Area School District.

continues

continued

    2. Transmitting any material in violation of any U.S. or state regulation or school board policy is prohibited. This includes, but is not limited to, copyrighted material and threatening or obscene material.

    3. Hate mail, harassment, discriminatory remarks, and other antisocial behaviors are unacceptable in Internet and other network communication.

    4. All information accessible via the Internet should be assumed to be private property and subject to copyright protection. Internet sources should be credited appropriately, as with the use of any copyrighted material. See, for instance *The Columbia Guide to Online Style*: <http://www.columbia.edu/cu/cup/cgos/idx_basic.html>

    5. Users have a responsibility to respect the privacy and property of other users. Users should not intentionally seek information about, obtain copies of, or modify files, data, or passwords of other users.

    6. For their own safety, users should not reveal any personal information, such as addresses, phone numbers, or photographs.

    7. Employing the Internet for commercial purposes is prohibited.

    8. Users should not expect that files stored on district servers will always be private. School and network administrators may review files and communications to maintain system integrity and to ensure that the network is being used responsibly.

    Teachers will inform students of what is considered appropriate use of the Internet, describing student privileges, rights, and responsibilities. As much as possible, teachers will guide students toward materials that have been reviewed and evaluated prior to use. The use of home pages, bookmarks, lists of web sites, and cataloging web sites in the library system will help match Internet resources to the curriculum.

    Because computer use is essentially an individual experience, however, primary responsibility for appropriate use of the Internet resides with the student. A user agreement form will be signed by the student and parent prior to their use. Failure to follow appropriate practices may result in disciplinary action, including loss of the individual's access to the Internet.

    Principals will supervise the use of the Internet and other computer networks in their schools. Procedures will be put in place to ensure that students receive appropriate instruction and supervision in the use of the Internet and other computer networks.

explicit pictures as well as harassing, defaming, and stalking other students. Material that disparages or harasses another student and is posted by a peer to a bulletin board can be particularly damaging and painful. For this reason, it is important for acceptable use policies to include rules making young people responsible for the content they create.

For an acceptable use policy to be effective, it must be communicated clearly to students and parents, it must come with consequences, and violations of the policies must be disciplined. It also needs to distinguish accidental viewing from deliberate seeking of inappropriate material. The former is best treated as an opportunity to educate the user about how to avoid such content in the future, how to remove it from their screen, and if necessary how to report it to the Internet service provider. A student who intentionally seeks inappropriate material would potentially be dealt with by some stated disciplinary action (e.g., loss of Internet privileges, call to parents, detention).

Linda Roberts noted that acceptable use policies are most effective when they are developed in conjunction with parents, community members, teachers, and students. Acceptable use policies developed jointly with the school and the community are more likely to incorporate the particular sensibilities of parents and can be designed to address specific concerns. One community, for example, may be more concerned about accidental exposure to sexually explicit material, while others worry about young people spending time in chat rooms. The process offers an opportunity for the community to consider the balance they want to try to strike between unregulated access to information or a more restricted use of the Internet. Such discourse can prevent future tensions between teachers and parents by allowing difficult and potentially contentious issues to be resolved.

Acceptable use policies can be effective in addressing not only sexually explicit material and content posted by students, but also other inappropriate material. These policies are low in cost for institutions, and although they require some effort initially to design, they are neither time- nor labor-intensive to maintain. The challenge in acceptable use policies lies in the extent to which they are clearly communicated to young people and then enforced.

RESPONSIBLE NETIZENSHIP: KNOWING WHEN AND HOW TO TAKE ACTION

Workshop participants noted that young people need to know what action to take if they have a problematic online experience. Nancy Willard described this skill set as "responsible netizenship." Willard emphasized the importance of providing young people with action- or response-oriented knowledge that would allow them to recognize and deal effectively with unsafe strangers, online predators, hate group recruiters, and sexual come-ons. They must also learn to recognize when they might be vulnerable and what steps to take in problematic situations. For example, she described the typical process through which both sexual predators and hate group recruiters generally approach young people. They try to get as much personal information as possible and then start feeding them "candy" in the form of compliments. This may seem a simplistic and obvious strategy, but a young person—like many unsuspecting adults—may not be impervious to flattery. If the young user responds that they do not have many friends, the next comment might be "that is hard to believe," or "your peers are really missing out, but you are probably too mature for them," and so on. Young people need to understand explicitly how this process works, what to expect, how to recognize it, and how to deal with the situation. For example, an appropriate response would be for young people to contact their Internet service provider or to be encouraged to be assertive online in terms of ending contact with another user or declining instant messages from users who harass them.

Training in how to be a responsible netizen could come as a part of media and information literacy training, parent educational outreach on children's Internet safety, or as a part of acceptable use policies (e.g., a policy could state that in addition to expecting that young people will avoid sexually explicit material, they are encouraged and expected to take appropriate action if they have an unpleasant encounter with another user). Like other forms of training, feasibility depends on having time in school curricula, funding to offer training in other community settings, and a communication strategy that can bring this issue to the attention of parents, teachers, and other adults. Responsible netizenship is also primarily designed to address experiences in which young people are having problematic instances with other users rather than being exposed to inappropriate web sites.

PROFESSIONAL DEVELOPMENT

Providing training to teachers, librarians, and parents to increase their efficacy with the Internet in particular and technology in general was noted as another important area for development. Linda Roberts was particularly concerned with the training offered to teachers as a part of becoming certified to teach as well as opportunities for professional development. Curriculum associated with certification should be reformed to include course work on various types of technologies, how to integrate them into the classroom effectively, and how to encourage a productive use of the Internet with a group of students. Roberts also wanted to see the number of professional development opportunities increased so that already-certified teachers have training opportunities to make them skillful users of technology and adept at incorporating technology into their curricula.

Mary Dempsey noted the importance of providing technology training to librarians and stated that ongoing training can be an opportunity not only to increase librarians skill with technology, but to also provide a venue for sharing strategies to keep young people on task with productive use of the Internet. Less formalized training in the form of regular meetings among librarians can offer the opportunity for individuals to share new information on technology (e.g., a newly discovered web site that is particularly good) as well as to discuss emerging issues and how to handle them. This less formalized training or knowledge sharing can help to disseminate new strategies individuals have found to be particularly effective in protecting young patrons from inappropriate material.

5

Research, Policy, and Practice: Future Directions

What research is needed to improve young people's online experiences, and what policies can help to make cyberspace safer for young people? Ellen Wartella, dean and professor of communication at the University of Texas at Austin, described a research agenda that would considerably broaden what is known about children and the Internet, while Betty Chemers, deputy administrator of the Justice Department's Office of Juvenile Justice and Delinquency Prevention (OJJDP), presented the policy consideration from a law enforcement perspective.

RESEARCH AGENDA TOPICS

Supporting informed policy decisions and better educational practices. Wartella identified several areas in which increased or improved research could greatly aid in making informed policy decisions and improve practices directed at educating parents and children about the Internet. These areas included research on networked environments, empirical studies of the impact of media content on young people, tracking studies, developmentally appropriate research, and studies to develop media literacy curricula as critical components in this research plan. Wartella also briefly discussed the role of federal, foundation, and industry funding of these types of research in advancing the body of knowledge in these fields.

Building the knowledge base on networked environments. According to Wartella, not enough research is being conducted on networked environments, and the knowledge base that could inform policy and practice is lagging well behind Internet growth and changes in the ways that young people use and access the Internet. Wartella also stated that there is a great need to regularly reconceptualize what constitutes networked environments and the media, and new research endeavors must be attentive to significant online changes. Current notions of the media as distinct platforms—such as television, radio, movies, print media—must be rethought now that material previously available on only one platform is accessible on the Internet. As new technologies offer additional means to access the Internet (e.g., cell phones and video games that connect to the Internet) and penetrate the population, it is likely that media platforms and communication forms will continue to collapse, and this has significant implications for research. For example, one implication of this collapsing of platforms is that the digital divide as it is currently defined—namely in terms of access to the Internet—will cease to be a relevant concept. Platforms like video games are found much more equally across socioeconomic and ethnic groups than are computers in the home, so games that access the Internet will greatly increase overall Internet access. However, a digital divide may continue to exist if there are great differences in the way young people use the Internet (e.g., for socializing and gaming or for research and homework help). Future research must consider the meaning of concepts like the digital divide to ensure that they are relevant to the current media and technological landscape.

The collapsing of media platforms is also relevant to policies that seek to regulate media content. Current theories of regulation are delineated by media platform. For example, First Amendment protections for print media are very strong compared with those regulating television and the radio; as Wartella noted, this is largely because society views radio and television airwaves as being owned by the public. Furthermore, she observed that a larger theoretical and philosophical understanding of what media are and in what ways media platforms intersect with regulatory policies represents foundational questions that should underlie future explorations of this topic.

Empirical studies on impact of media content. Future research on the media should also focus on the impact of content on young people, seeking to answer questions about how they learn about sexuality from the media, as well as how vulnerable or resistant they are to the messages conveyed through inappropriate content. Such research should focus attention especially on the media exposure young people receive at home, as past research has emphasized the use of media for educational purposes in school environments. In addition, research should also examine the nature of role and identity playing that young people can experience in networked environment.

Adopting a developmental approach. Applied and basic research that is developmental in nature must be a part of scholarly inquiry into the media. Wartella stressed that funding basic research, whose implication for policy and practice may not be immediately apparent at the time of the research, may well prove to be extremely important to policy. For example, the American Academy of Pediatrics in 1999 recommended that no child under the age of 2 be put in front of a screen (television, computer, or any other). Currently, there is no research to support this recommendation. Basic research on a topic such as the neuropsychological consequences of young children viewing a screen is essential to developing policy such as that recommended by the American Academy of Pediatrics. This research could determine what effects screen exposure may have on very young children and at what age—be it younger or older than age 2—and what length of exposure is safe for this age group. In addition, basic research to evaluate the effectiveness of filters (e.g., how accurate are they in terms of screening inappropriate content while not blocking appropriate sites), as well as the extent to which children and parents use filters is also important.

New tracking studies could be a sourceof developmental information. Developmental tracking studies represent another important source of information about children's media habits as well as their potential impact. Wartella identified the Panel Study of Income Dynamics (PSID), a longitudinal survey of a representative sample of U.S. individuals and their families, as an opportunity to collect tracking data about children's media use. Data from this survey can be used for cross-sectional, longitudinal, and intergenerational analysis, all of which would greatly help to develop this field of knowledge. Tracking studies such as PSID provide data on such influences on children's development as peers, family income, and education. According to Wartella, the media is a powerful source of socialization in children's lives, and it is extremely problematic not to be collecting tracking data. Funding is a considerable impediment to gathering these data, and the support of both foundations and the federal government is needed for such projects.

Developing media literacy curriculum. Wartella emphasized the need for research on media literacy to determine if, how, and what types of skills may protect against some of the harmful messages contained in the media. This research should be used to develop effective programs and curricula and these programs should become a part of school curriculum. Wartella noted that unlike England, New Zealand, Australia, parts of Africa, and Canada, the United States is the only large English-speaking country that has no regular media literacy curriculum. In this respect, the United States lags behind other countries in developing effective media literacy curriculum and a research base to support the creation of these programs.

Role of federal, foundation, and industry funding. Research supported by federal, foundation, and industry funding that is developmental in nature has the potential to produce information that would assist in developing effective policy, as well as the type of socially appropriate, beneficial, and educational media content that many workshop participants stated is lacking on the Internet currently. Wartella noted that Sesame Street—an icon of the educational potential of television—was developed largely through developmental research supported by the Markle Foundation. A similar approach could be taken to research on Internet content, with the intention of producing informed policy and outstanding programming for children.

In addition to the potential of funding research projects that would translate readily into practices (e.g., media literacy) and educational products (e.g., Sesame Street-type programming for the Internet), Wartella stated that there is a great need for ongoing funding for research on children's media use. This need stems in large part from the importance of identifying emerging patterns of children's Internet use in order to stay abreast of new ways that young people may be influenced by the media. Federal funding is essential to this, according to Wartella, because it stimulates systematic research that becomes cumulative over time.

INTERNET POLICY FROM A LAW ENFORCEMENT PERSPECTIVE

While Wartella centered her comments on needed research and what policy and practice might extend from this research agenda, Betty Chemers discussed policy from the perspective of law enforcement. OJJDP approaches the regulation of Internet content by encouraging self-regulation by the industry; supporting nonprofit organizations in developing child-friendly, high-quality content and technological tools to help parents protect children; encouraging public institutions offering Internet services to adopt acceptable use policies; and strongly supporting the enforcement of existing laws that prohibit the distribution of child pornography and the use of the Internet to entice or lure children into dangerous situations with the potential for abuse.

As a part of the department's law enforcement of Internet crimes, 30 task forces were created to provide forensic, prevention, and investigative assistance to parents, educational institutions, prosecutors, and local law enforcement. A cyber tipline that is being coordinated through the National Center for Missing and Exploited Children was also developed so that Internet users can report suspicious online activity, and the department is also working with other countries to develop technologies and coordinate law enforcement efforts to protect minors rather than to increase government censorship of Internet material. Box 5-1 provides additional information on the CyberTipLine and the National Center for Missing and Exploited Children.

At the time of the workshop, OJJDP was in the process of finishing a report to identify strategies to protect children online. According to Chemers, its recommendations were consistent with the Commission on Child Online Protection's report to Congress (2000). Chemers highlighted several policy-oriented strategies that are particularly relevant in thinking about nontechnical strategies. The COPA report states that the most effective means of protecting children is through aggressive efforts for public education, consumer empowerment, increased resources for the enforcement of existing laws, and greater use of existing technologies (see Box 5-2 for a summary of that report's recommendations). In addition to these approaches, important steps to pursue in protecting young people online include browsers featuring a prominently displayed parental control button, increased industry self-regulation and voluntary standards or labeling that help to restrict minors' access to pornography, and age verification technology. Further research involving third party testing of the effectiveness of filtering and blocking technologies would also be important as these technologies can be costly to implement on a wide-scale basis.

A related joint activity of OJJDP and the Federal Trade Commission involves an analysis of whether the movie, music, recording, and computer and video game industries are marketing and advertising products with violent content to young people. This analysis concluded that these industries do indeed promote to young people content that the industries have themselves identified as warranting parental caution, and their advertisements are

BOX 5-1
National Center for Missing and Exploited Children's CyberTipLine

In 1984 the National Center for Missing and Exploited Children (NCMEC) was founded to serve as a focal point in providing assistance to parents, children, law enforcement, schools, and the community in recovering missing children and raising public awareness about ways to help prevent child abduction, molestation, and sexual exploitation. One area that has been of growing concern for NCMEC is children's safety online. The U.S. Census Bureau estimates that roughly 14 million children use the Internet—2 million children use the Internet at both home and school while about 7 million children access the Internet only at school (U.S. Bureau of the Census, 1999a, 1999b). Although the majority of children use the Internet safely, concern that the Internet could be used as a tool to exploit children spurred Congress to provide funding and support for the CyberTipLine.

In conjunction with the Federal Bureau of Investigation, the U.S. Customs Service, and the U.S. Postal Inspection Service, the NCMEC initiated the development of the CyberTipLine in 1998 to provide a vehicle to report and reduce incidences of child sexual exploitation. The CyberTipLine collects information on the following types of incidents involving children and the Internet:

- Possession, manufacture, and distribution of child pornography,
- Child sexual molestation (extrafamilial child sexual abuse),
- Online enticement of children for sexual acts,
- Child prostitution, and
- Child-sex tourism.

The NCMEC's Exploited Child Unit manages the CyberTipLine. This unit processes and analyzes incident reports and then submits report information to law enforcement officials for further investigation. According to NCMEC, since its inception through August 2000, the CyberTipLine has received over 24,000 incident reports. About 19,000 of these reports involved child pornography. The NCMEC reports receiving over 20,000 leads, many of which resulted in arrests.

Reports of child sexual exploitation can be filed online at <www.CyberTipLine.com> or by calling the toll free number, 1-800-843-5678. Information on the National Center for Missing and Exploited Children can be found at <www.missingkids.com>.

> **BOX 5-2**
> **Commission on Child Online Protection**
>
> In October 1998 Congress established the Commission on Online Child Protection to study methods to reduce access by minors to sexually explicit material on the Internet. These technologies and methods were evaluated on the basis of accessibility, cost, effectiveness, impact on First Amendment values, and implications for law enforcement. The commission concluded that no single approach would effectively screen children from this material, but that a combination of increased public awareness, accessible consumer technologies and methods, increased enforcement of existing laws, and industry self-regulation could have a significant effect. The commission published the following abbreviated version of its recommendations in the executive summary of its report:
>
> Public Education: (1) Government and the private sector should undertake a major education campaign to promote public awareness of technologies and methods available to protect children online. (2) Government and industry should effectively promote acceptable use policies.
>
> Consumer Empowerment Efforts: (1) Resources should be allocated for the independent evaluation of child protection technologies and to provide reports to the public about the capabilities of these technologies. (2) Industry should take steps to improve child protection mechanisms, and make them more accessible online. (3) A broad, national, private-sector conversation should be encour-

intended to attract children and teenagers. Recommendations from this report include the expansion of industry codes prohibiting targeted marketing to children and the inclusion of sanctions for violations; an extension of industry self-regulation to the retail level, such as the development of advisory labels that would discourage sales to children under a certain age; developing guidelines for the electronic transfer of movies, music, and games; and finally, increased industry efforts to raise parental awareness of the ratings and labeling systems currently available. Chemers stated that although this report focused on computer games, music, and movies, its recommendations are certainly relevant to any discussion of Internet content.

aged on the development of next-generation systems for labeling, rating, and identifying content reflecting the convergence of old and new media. (4) Government should encourage the use of technology in efforts to make children's experience of the Internet safe and useful.

Law Enforcement: (1) Government at all levels should fund, with significant new money, aggressive programs to investigate, prosecute, and report violations of federal and state obscenity laws, including efforts that emphasize the protection of children from accessing materials illegal under current state and federal obscenity law. (2) State and federal law enforcement should make available a list, without images, of Usenet newsgroup, IP addresses, World Wide Web sites, or other Internet sources that have been found to contain child pornography or where convictions have been obtained involving obscene material. (3) Federal agencies, pursuant to further congressional rulemaking authority as needed, should consider greater enforcement and possibly rulemaking to discourage deceptive or unfair practices that entice children to view obscene materials, including the practices of "mousetrapping" and deceptive metatagging. (4) Government should provide new money to address international aspects of Internet crime, including both obscenity and child pornography.

Industry Action: (1) The ISP industry should voluntarily undertake "best practices" to protect minors. (2) The online commercial adult industry should voluntarily take steps to restrict minors' ready access to adult content.

6

Developing Nontechnical Strategies: Concluding Thoughts

The Workshop on Nontechnical Strategies brought together a group of experts from a diverse group of fields and broad set of expertise, including developmental psychologists, researchers in communication and the media, policy makers, educators, and practitioners who have developed strategies to provide young people with positive Internet experiences. Several points were reiterated throughout the workshop, and participants' comments converged on several topics.

Researchers emphasized that there are a very limited number of studies on the impact of the sexually explicit media content on children. This lack of research makes it impossible to come to any definitive conclusions about the media's potential impact, and they cautioned against succumbing to a sense of panic that has historically accompanied new media developments and that they observed occurring around the topic of young people encountering sexually explicit material online. An approach driven by what we know about children's developmental needs rather than fear would serve to generate effective strategies. More research to gather basic information about children's Internet and media consumption as well as studies to identify the impact on cognitive, social, and emotional development of various types of media content would aid in the creation of appropriate policy for young people's Internet use and activities.

Although a critical research base on the impact of media content is not yet available, strategies to provide young people with positive and enriching Internet experiences can be developed from a scientific understanding of the developmental needs and milestones of children. Existing research on the cognitive, social, emotional, and moral development of young people represents a great resource that could be used to create educational and stimulating Internet content, serving both to meet the developmental needs of young people and prevent them from encountering inappropriate material by offering enticing and beneficial alternatives.

Workshop participants noted in particular that increasing the amount and availability of online, educational content addressing healthy sexuality and sexual health would be of particular benefit to young people for those times when they turn to the media for answers to questions about sexuality that they do not or are unwilling to ask adults. Currently, the amount of sexual health information is limited, especially in light of the vast amount of pornography and other sexually explicit material online. Balancing these ratios could be very helpful to young people.

In addition to creating age appropriate Internet content, developmental psychology can also be used to generate programs to educate young users about Internet use and the media. The workshop featured several examples of age and developmentally appropriate educational programs, for example, the Wisconsin schools' Internet-related educational objectives that students had to meet by the end of certain years, and teach such skills as effective searching and how to evaluate online content for truthfulness and validity.

Media and information literacy were identified by virtually every speaker as having great potential for protecting children from a wide range of inappropriate material. Information literacy can prevent young people from accidentally coming in contact with inappropriate content by teaching them how to find information effectively and to recognize a problematic web site or email before viewing it. Media literacy combined with the principles of responsible netizenship and Internet safety training offers a comprehensive set of critical thinking skills to aid young people in assessing the value of Internet content and interactions with other users in order to make sound decisions about how to handle that material—be it to exit the site or report an inappropriate site, interaction, or solicitation to the Internet service provider or to decline from citing misinformation as a valid source of knowledge.

Educating parents and children on Internet safety was also emphasized, and comments converged on the need for a public awareness campaign to raise parents' awareness of the importance of talking with their children about appropriate online conduct and safety. Greater dissemination and public awareness of tools and programs already available to parents were also noted as useful strategies. For example, parents may not think to look for online resources providing information on filters (e.g., the GetNetWise web site), and may not have heard about the suggestions on The Children's Partnership web site on strategies they can use at home to guide their children's Internet use. Parents may also not know about the educational programs offered by their local libraries or by nonprofit groups in their area and may be missing other opportunities to receive training and assistance in this issue.

In general, workshop participants voiced the view that parents should consider carefully children's exposure to sexually explicit and other inappropriate material and develop approaches that reflected their concerns and values. Participants observed that fearful responses were not advisable as they often prevent adults from developing a well-considered approach to this issue, but they viewed educating parents and other adults about the risks as an important step in dealing with this issue. Sexually explicit material is one of a number of types of content that can be targeted in choosing nontechnical strategies, participants noted, and web sites are only one way for young people to encounter sexually explicit material. Adults should be mindful of how interactive sites such as chat rooms and instant messaging should figure in well-considered approaches. Finally, workshop participants noted that attention to the multiple contexts (e.g., school, home, unsupervised Internet cafés) and platforms (e.g., desktop computers, laptops, portable phones) should also be considered as adults develop strategies to protect young people.

References

For a list of web sites listed in the text, see the end of this reference list.

Alemi, F., Alemagno, S.A., Goldhagen, J., Ash, L., Finkelstein, B., Lavin, A., Butts, J., & Ghadiri, A. (1996). Computer reminders improve on-time immunization rates. *Medical Care, 34*(suppl 10), 0S45-51.

Alemi, F., Cherry, F., & Meffret, G. (1989). Rehearsing decisions may help teenagers: An evaluation of a simulation game. *Computer Biological Medicine, 19,* 283-290.

Becker, Henry Jay. (2000). Who's wired and who's not: Children's access to and use of computer technology. *The Future of Children and Computer Technology, 10*(2), 44-75.

Brown, J.D., Childers, K.W., & Waszak, C.S. (1990). Television and adolescent sexuality. *Journal of Adolescent Health Care, 11,* 62-70.

Brown, J.D., & Newcomer, S. (1991). Television viewing and adolescents' sexual behavior. *Journal of Homosexuality, 21*(1/2), 77-91.

Brown, J.D., & Stern, S. (in press). Sex and the media. In *Encyclopedia of communication and information.* New York: Macmillan.

Calvert, S.L. (1999). *Children's journeys through the information age.* Boston: McGraw Hill.

Calvert, S.L., & Tan, S. (1994). Impact of virtual reality on young adults' physiological arousal and aggressive thoughts: Interaction versus observation. *Journal of Applied Developmental Psychology, 15,* 125-139.

Cantor, J. (1998). *"Mommy, I'm scared": How TV and movies frighten children and what we can do to protect them.* San Diego, CA: Harcourt Brace.

Cantor, J. (2000). Media violence and children's emotions: Beyond the "Smoking gun." Paper presented at the annual convention of the American Psychological Association, Washington, D.C. [Online] Available: <http://joannecantor.com/EMOTIONS2_sgl.htm.>

Cantor, J., Mares, M.L., & Oliver, M.B. (1993). Parents' and children's emotional reactions to televised coverage of the Gulf War. In B. Greenberg & W. Gantz (Eds.), *Desert Storm and the mass media* (pp. 325-340). Cresskill, NJ: Hampton Press.

Carlson, L., Grossbart, S., & Stuenke, J.K. (1992). The role of parental socialization types on differential family communication patterns regarding consumption. *Journal of Consumer Psychology, 1*(1), 31-52.

Carnegie Corporation of New York. (1996, September). *Years of promise: A comprehensive learning strategy for America's children.* New York, NY: Author.

Cline, V.B., Croft, R.G., & Courrier, S. (1973). Desensitization of children to television violence. *Journal of Personality and Social Psychology, 27,* 516-546.

Commission on Child Online Protection. (2000, October). Final Report to Congress. Transmitted to Congress, October 20, 2000. Washington, DC. [Online] Available: <http://www.copacommission.org/report/>

Damon, W. (1988). *The moral child.* New York: Free Press.

Donnerstein, E.I., & Linz, D.G. (1986). Mass media sexual violence and male viewers: Current theory and research. *American Behavioral Scientist, 29,* 601-618.

Dunn, J. (1987). The beginnings of moral understanding. In J. Kagan & S. Lamb (Eds.), *The emergence of morality in young children.* Chicago: University of Chicago Press.

Greenson, L., & Williams, R.A. (1986). Social implications of music videos for youth: An analysis of the content and effects of MTV. *Youth & Society, 18*(2), 177-189.

Harrison, K., & Cantor, J. (1999). Tales from the screen: Enduring fright reactions to scary media. *Media Psychology, 1,* 117-140.

Heinberg, L.J., & Thompson, J.K. (1995). Body image and televised images of thinness and attractiveness: A controlled laboratory investigation. *Journal of Social and Clinical Psychology, 14,* 325-338.

Hofschire, L., & Greenberg, B. (2001). Media's impact on adolescents' body dissatisfaction. In J.D. Brown, J.R. Steele, & K. Walsh-Childers (Eds.), *Sexual teens, sexual media.* Hillsdale, NJ: Lawrence Erlbaum Associates.

Huston, A.C., Wartella, E., & Donnerstein, E. (1998). *Measuring the effects of sexual content in the media: A report to the Kaiser Family Foundation.* Menlo Park, CA: The Henry J. Kaiser Family Foundation.

Kalof, L. (1999). The effects of gender and music video imagery on sexual attitudes. *The Journal of Social Psychology, 139*(3), 378-366.

Kapoun, J. (2000). *Criteria for evaluating web sites.* Washington, DC: American Library Association.

Keller, S. (2000). *How do early adolescent girls use media to shape their romantic identities?* Unpublished doctoral dissertation, University of North Carolina, Chapel Hill.

Keller, S., Gilbert, L., & Short, J. (2000). *Phase 1 report case study: www.iwannaknow.org content analyses.* Unpublished manuscript.

Keller, S., Labelle, H., Karimi, N., & Gupta, S. (2001). STD prevention for teenagers: A look at the Internet universe. Paper presented at the 20th annual meeting of the Association for Health Care Research, Santa Fe, NM.

Kerr, M., & Statin, H. (2000). What parents know; how they know it; & several forms of adolescent adjustment: Further support for a reinterpretation of monitoring. *Developmental Psychology, 36,* 366-380.

Kraak, V., & Pelletier, D. (1998). How marketers reach young consumers: Implications for nutrition education and health promotion campaigns. *Family Economics and Nutrition Review, 11*(4), 31.

Krafka, C., Linz, D., Donnerstein, E., & Penrod, S. (1997). Women's reactions to sexually aggressive mass media depictions. *Violence Against Women, 3*, 149-181.

Larson, M. (1996). Sex roles and soap operas: What adolescents learn about single motherhood. *Sex Roles: A Journal of Research, 35*(1/2), 97-121.

Lemish, D. (1997). The school as a wrestling arena: The modeling of a television series. *Communication, 22*(4), 395-418.

Levine, M.D., Carey, W.B., Crocker, A.C., & Gross, R.T. (1983*). Developmental-behavioral pediatrics*. Philadelphia: W.B. Saunders Company.

Linz, D.G., Donnerstein, E.I., & Adams, S.M. (1989). Physiological desensitization and judgments about female victims of violence. *Human Communication Research, 15*, 509-522.

Linz, D.G., Donnerstein, E.I., & Penrod, S. (1988). Effects of long-term exposure to violent and sexually degrading depictions of women. *Journal of Personality & Social Psychology, 55*, 758-768.

Locke, S.E., Kowaloff, H.B., Hoff, R.G., Safran, C., Popovsky, M.A., & Cotton, D.J. (1992) Computer-based interview for screening blood donors for risk of HIV transmission. *Journal of the American Medical Association, 268*, 1301-1305.

Mangleburg, T., & Bristol, T. (1998). Socializing and adolescents' skepticism toward advertising. *Journal of Advertising, 27*(3). [Special issue on advertising to children].

Molitor, F., & Hirsch, K.W. (1994). Children's toleration of real-life aggression after exposure to media violence: A replication of the Drabman and Thomas studies. *Child Study Journal, 24*, 191-207.

Mullin, C.R., & Linz, D. (1995). Desensitization and resensitization to violence against women: Effects of exposure to sexually violent films on judgments of domestic violence victims. *Journal of Personality and Social Psychology, 69*, 449-459.

Nathanson, A.I., & Cantor, J. (2000). Reducing the aggression-promoting effect of violent cartoons by increasing children's fictional involvement with the victim. *Journal of Broadcasting & Electronic Media, 44*, 125-142.

National Center for Health Statistics. (1995). *Trends in pregnancies and pregnancy rates, 1980-1992: Estimates for the U.S.* (National Survey of Family Growth, Monthly Vital Statistics Report, 43—11, supplement). Hyattsville, MD: Author.

National Center for Health Statistics. (1999). *Declines in teenage birth rates, 1991-1998: Update on national and state trends.* (National Vital Statistics Report, Vol. 47, No. 26). Hyattsville, MD: Author.

National Research Council and Institute of Medicine. (2000). *From neurons to neighborhoods: The science of early childhood development.* Committee on Integrating the Science of Early Childhood Development. Jack P. Shonkoff and Deborah A. Phillips, eds. Board on Children, Youth, and Families, Commission on Behavioral and Social Sciences and Education. Washington, DC: National Academy Press.

National School Boards Association. (n.d.) Safe & smart: Overview of research and guidelines for children's use of the Internet. National School Boards Association. [Online] Available: <http://www.nsbf.org/safe-smart/key.htm>

Novak, T.P., & Hoffman, D.L. (1998). *Bridging the digital divide: The impact of race on computer access and internet use.* [Online] Available: <http://www2000.ogsm.vanderbilt.edu/papers/race/science.html>

Odlyzko, A. (2000, November 22). Internet growth: Myth and reality, use and abuse. *iMP Magazine*. [Online] Available: <http://www.cisp.org/imp/november_2000/odlyzko/11_00odlyzko.htm>

Owens, J., Maxim, R., McGuinn, M., Nobile, C., Msall, M., & Alario, A. (1999). Television-viewing habits and sleep disturbance in school children. *Pediatrics, 104* (3), 552 (Abstract). [Online] Available: <http://www.pediatrics.org/cgi/content/full/104/3/c27>

Pardun, C. (2001). Romancing the script: Identifying the romantic agenda in top-grossing movies. In J.D. Borwn, J.R. Steele, & K.W. Childers (Eds.), *Sexual teens, sexual media.* Hillsdale, NJ: Lawrence Erlbaum Associates.

Penn, Schoen & Berland Associates. (2000, September). Web savvy and safety: How kids and parents differ in what they know, whom they trust. [Online] Available: <http://www.microsoft.com/PressPass/press/2000/Nov00/SafetyWebsitesPR.asp>

Public Broadcasting Service. (n.d.) *Life on the Internet: Timeline.* [PBS Online] Available: <http://www.pbs.org/internet/timeline/index.html>

Richardson, F. (2000, November 27). Study: Millions log onto Net to get health information. *Boston Herald.*

Roberts, Donald F., Foehr, Ulla G., Rideout, Victoria J., and Mollyann Brodie. (1999). *Kids and media at the new millennium: A comprehensive national analysis of children's media use.* Menlo Park, CA: The Henry J. Kaiser Family Foundation.

Signorielli, N. (1991). Adolescents and ambivalence toward marriage: A cultivation analysis. *Youth and Society, 23*(1), 11-25.

Singer, J.L., & Singer, D.G. (1993). *A study of children's media usage in relationship to reading, math, and computer study in an elementary school.* Monograph prepared for the Corporation for Public Broadcasting. Yale University Family Television Research and Consultation Center, New Haven, CT.

Singer, M.I., Slovak, K., Frierson, T., & York, P. (1998). Viewing preferences, symptoms of psychological trauma, and violent behaviors among children who watch television. *Journal of the American Academy of Child and Adolescent Psychiatry, 37,* 1041-1048.

Smith, M., Gertz, E., Alvarez, S., & Lurie, P. (2000). The content and accessibility of sex education information on the Internet. *Health Education & Behavior, 27*(6), 684-694.

Steinberg, L. (1999). *Adolescence* (5th ed.). New York: McGraw-Hill.

Strasburger, V. (1989). Adolescent sexuality and the media. *Adolescent Gynecology, 36,* 747-773.

Strouse, J., Buerkel-Rothfuss, N. & Long, E.C. (1995). Gender and family as moderators of the relationship between music video exposure and adolescent sexual permissiveness. *Adolescence, 30,* 505-521.

Strouse, J., & Fabes, R.A. (1985). Formal versus informal informational sources of sex education: Competing forces in the sexual socialization of adolescents. *Adolescence, 20,* 251-263.

Survey on teen use of technology. (2000, October). *Family PC Magazine.*

Sutton, M., Brown, J.D., Wilson, K., & Klein, J. (2001). Shaking the tree of knowledge for forbidden fruit: Where adolescents learn about sexuality and contraception. In J.D. Brown, J.R. Steele, & K.W. Childers (Eds.), *Sexual teens, sexual media.* Hillsdale, NJ: Lawrence Erlbaum Associates.

U.S. Bureau of the Census. (1999a, October 14). Press release. [Online] Available: <http://www.census.gov/Press-Release/www/1999/cb99-194.html>

U.S. Bureau of the Census. (1999b). *Computer use in the United States: October 1997* (P20-522). [Online] Available: <http://www.census.gov/population/www/socdemo/computer.html>

Wartella, E., & Jennings, N. (2000). Children and computers: New technology—old concerns. *The Future of Children, 10*(2), 31-43.

Youniss, J. (1980). *Parents and peers in social development*. Chicago: University of Chicago Press.

Youniss, J., & Smollar, J. (1985). *Adolescent relations with mothers, fathers, and friends*. Chicago: University of Chicago Press.

Youniss, J., & Yates, M. (1999). Youth service and moral-civic identity: A case for everyday morality. *Educational Psychology Review, 11*(4), 363-378.

Zillmann, D. (1982). Transfer of excitation in emotional behavior. In J.T. Cacioppo & R.E. Petty (Eds.), *Social Psychophysiology*. New York: Guilford.

Zillmann, D., & Bryant, J. (1982). Pornography, sexual callousness, and the trivialization of rape. *Journal of Communication, 32*, 10-21.

Zillman, D., & Weaver, J.B. (1999). Effects of prolonged exposure to gratuitous media violence on provoked and unprovoked hostile behavior. *Journal of Applied Social Psychology, 29*, 145-165.

Zollo, P. (1995). Talking to teens. *American Demographics, 17*(November), 22-28.

REFERENCE OF WEB SITES LISTED IN THE TEXT

Web sites are listed in the order in which they appear at the text. All were current as of the time of the workshop.

Shared Experience Cancer Support Knowledgebase: www.sharedexperience.org
Grunwald Associates: www.grunwald.com/survey/index.htm
Chicago Public Library Sign of the Owl: www.chipublib.org/008subject/003cya/sign/sign.html
The Children's Partnership: www.childrenspartnership.org
Eau Claire Area School District's acceptable use policy: www.ecasd.k12.wi.us/departments/technology/network/inetpol.html
Columbia Guide to Online Style: http://www.columbia.edu/cu/cup/cgos/idx_basic.html
CyberTipLine: www.CyberTipLine.com
National Center for Missing and Exploited Children: www.missingkids.com

Appendix: Workshop Materials

WORKSHOP AGENDA

December 13, 2000

8:00 a.m. – 8:30 a.m.
Registration and Continental Breakfast

8:30 a.m. – 8:45 a.m.
Welcome, Introductions, and Purpose of the Workshop

    Richard Thornburgh, Committee and Workshop Chair

8:45 a.m. – 9:30 a.m.
Nontechnical Strategies That Can Be Used To Protect Children on the Internet: What are the Roles of Policies, Parents, Schools, Libraries, and Communities

    Linda Roberts, Director, Office of Educational Technology and Senior Adviser to the Secretary, U.S. Department of Education
    Anne Thompson, Program Commissioner, National PTA

    Q&A and General Discussion

- How does one define nontechnical strategies for protecting kids from inappropriate material on the Internet?

- What nontechnical approaches are used in the home, classroom, and community settings?
- What is the role of parents in making nontechnical strategies effective, and what do parents need?
- How effective have current policies been in encouraging schools and communities to develop nontechnical strategies?

9:30 a.m. – 9:45 a.m.
Short Break

9:45 a.m. – 12:00 p.m.
An Extended Panel on Bringing Developmental Considerations to Bear on the Impact of Inappropriate Material on the Internet

    Moderator/Discussant: Sandra Calvert, Committee Member and Professor of Psychology, Georgetown University

Format Note: Questions and open discussion will be held until after the second part of the panel.

Part I: Effects of Exposure to Pornographic and Other Inappropriate Material on the Internet

    Jane Brown, Professor, School of Journalism and Mass Communications, University of North Carolina at Chapel Hill
    Joanne Cantor, Professor, University of Wisconsin-Madison
    Ed Donnerstein, Dean and Professor, Department of Communication, University of California-Santa Barbara

- What types of inappropriate material do young people encounter, and how do they come in contact with it?
- What is the potential impact on children of viewing sexually explicit and other forms of inappropriate material in the media?
- Is impact dependent only on the type of material or also on the source (e.g., static image on the Internet, picture from a magazine, active images from television)?
- What are the limits of this research, and to what extent can we make comparisons among the effects of viewing different types of inappropriate material (e.g., sexually explicit vs. violent vs. hate speech)?

Part II: Developmental Considerations for Determining Appropriate Internet Use Guidelines for Children and Adolescents

> Patricia Greenfield, Professor, Department of Psychology, University of California at Los Angeles
> James Youniss, Professor, Life Cycle Institute, Catholic University of America
> Dorothy Singer, Senior Research Scientist, Department of Psychology, Yale University, and Co-director, Yale University Family Television Research and Consultation Center

- How are emotional, cognitive, social, and moral development affected by the media landscape created by children's access and use of the Internet?
- What types of material may be harmful according to children's growth and developmental needs, and how may harmful effects change with age and developmental milestone?
- How do parents and educators balance giving young people the responsibility of exploring the Internet with protecting them from material that may be disturbing?
- How should developmental issues shape nontechnical strategies to protect kids from inappropriate material, and what nontechnical strategies will most benefit children's development?

12:00 p.m. – 12:45 p.m.
Quick Lunch

12:45 p.m. – 1:45 p.m.
Push and Pull on the Internet: Children's Use and Experiences

> Don Roberts, Thomas More Storke Professor, Department of Communications, Stanford University
> Sarah Keller, Assistant Professor, Health Communication, Department of Communication, Emerson College
>
> Moderator/Discussant: Janet Schofield, Committee Member, Professor of Psychology and Senior Scientist at the Learning Research and Development Center, University of Pittsburgh

Q&A and General Discussion

- How are children using the Internet, in what settings are children logging on, and are there differential patterns of use according to age, gender, and ethnicity?
- What are children's experiences while online, both positive and negative?
- How are children pulled into material that they might not otherwise view, and what effect might this have?
- How are young people driving their experiences on the Internet, and how can young people be encouraged to stay in charge of their online experiences?

1:45 p.m. – 2:00 p.m.
Short Break

2:00 p.m. – 3:45 p.m.
Innovative Approaches and Existing Efforts to Use NonTechnological Strategies to Protect Children on the Internet

> Laurie Lipper, Director, The Children's Partnership
> Kathy Boguszewski, Instructional Technology Consultant, Wisconsin Department of Public Instruction
> Mary Dempsey, Commissioner, Chicago Public Library
> Nancy Willard, Director, Responsible Netizen Research, Center for Advanced Technology in Education, University of Oregon
> Eileen Faucette, Founder and Coordinator, PTA Live Online
>
> Moderator/Discussant: Winnie Wechsler, Committee Member

Q&A and General Discussion

- What are some of the nontechnological strategies that might be used by educators, librarians, parents, and local communities to ensure children's safe and appropriate use of the Internet?
- What types of inappropriate material do these strategies address, and how do they protect against the potential harm this material might cause?

- Who has been responsible for implementing and monitoring these approaches?
- How can these approaches be tailored to different venues (e.g., home, school, library)?

3:45 p.m. – 4:45 p.m.
Bridging Research, Policy, and Practice

> Ellen Wartella, Dean and Professor, College of Communication, University of Texas-Austin
> Betty Chemers, Deputy Administrator, Office of Juvenile Justice and Delinquency Prevention

> *Q&A and General Discussion*

- What research is needed to develop new nontechnical strategies for protecting children from inappropriate material on the Internet?
- Are regulations needed to protect children on the Internet, and what policies might encourage children to use the Internet in safe and appropriate ways?
- How are and how should nonprofit organizations, educational institutions, government agencies, and parents work together to create a safe environment for kids to use the Internet?
- How should we be thinking about linking research, policy, and practice?

4:45 p.m.
Concluding Remarks

> Richard Thornburgh, Committee and Workshop Chair

5:00 p.m.
Adjourn

PRESENTERS

Kathy Boguszewski, Wisconsin Department of Public Instruction, Madison
Jane Brown, School of Journalism and Mass Communication, University of North Carolina-Chapel Hill
Joanne Cantor, University of Wisconsin-Madison
Betty Chemers, Office of Juvenile Justice and Delinquency Prevention, U.S. Department of Justice, Washington, DC
Mary Dempsey, Chicago Public Library
Ed Donnerstein, Department of Communication, University of California-Santa Barbara
Eileen Faucette, PTA Live Online, Augusta, GA
Patricia Greenfield, Department of Psychology, University of California-Los Angeles
Sarah Keller, Department of Communication, Emerson College
Laurie Lipper, The Children's Partnership, Washington, DC
Donald Roberts, Department of Communication, Stanford University
Linda Roberts, Office of Educational Technology, U.S. Department of Education, Washington, DC
Dorothy Singer, Yale University Family Television Research and Consultation Center, Yale University
Anne Thompson, National PTA, Miami, FL
Ellen Wartella, College of Communication, University of Texas at Austin
Nancy Willard, Center for Advanced Technology in Education, University of Oregon
James Youniss, Life Cycle Institute, Catholic University